AN EAGLE SOARS

One Man's Journey To Baldness

BY TURNEY HALL

A POST HILL PRESS book

ISBN (Hardcover): 978-1-61868-9-610
ISBN (eBook): 978-1-61868-9-627

An Eagle Soars copyright © 2014
by Turney Hall
All Rights Reserved.
Cover art by Ryan Truso

This book is a work of fiction. People, places, events, and situations are the product of the author's imagination. Any resemblance to actual persons, living or dead, or historical events, is purely coincidental.

No part of this book may be reproduced, stored in a retrieval system, or transmitted by any means without the written permission of the author and publisher.

To my parents, Bob and Colleen, my wife, Aisling, and my boy, Moseley

It's settled. The next time I go to the barbershop I am asking for, *nay*, demanding "The Anton Chigurh." It may be my last chance, and I want to punctuate my final days with an exclamation point. No, I'm not dying. But a part of me is, slowly. For the past several years, I have been fighting an inevitable descent into the genetic abyss known as male pattern baldness. I am certainly not alone in this fight, but sometimes it feels like I am. I have suffered silently, like a teenager who foolishly wears tight jeans during his first lap dance at the local strip club. And sometimes, like that foolish boy, I feel like waiving a white flag and asking for a do-over. However, there are no second chances in the baldness community, only disturbing cover-ups like toupees, hair plugs, and berets. So, I will not give up or give in. Instead, I will hold my head up high. I will no longer remain silent and I will pick a different fight - if not for myself, then for the rest of the baldness community. But just like Jesus had Peter and Paul, I need my own disciples. There is strength in numbers, and together we shall let the world know that we may be losing our hair, but we are still human beings.

It has been many years since I have had a regular barber. From my first haircut at age three until I graduated from college, I went to a place called Rialto's in Princeton, New Jersey. Rialto's was run by two Italian-American gents, Ed and Rich. Like me, Ed and Rich were faithful followers of the New York Mets, so we always had something to complain about while they made me look respectable.

I liked going to Rialto's, especially when puberty started knocking on my door. You see, as proprietors of a barbershop, Ed and Rich's clientele was exclusively male, so they knew how to treat their customers. From what I remember, Rialto's was a booming business, and there was always a line. But from the time I was twelve, I didn't care about the long wait. Instead, I welcomed it. Without fail, the magazine table at Rialto's was stocked with the latest issues of *Penthouse* and *Playboy*. Hello, Miss August!

But there was a system. It wasn't a great system, but a system nonetheless. Because women like my mom came into Rialto's every so often to make sure their sons didn't get a mohawk or a mullet, if you "read" a gentlemen's magazine such as *Playboy* while you waited in line, you had to put the *Playboy* inside a mother-friendly magazine like *Time* or *People*. So, even if you were checking out the measurements of Miss August instead of catching up on the starvation crisis in Ethiopia or taking in a fascinating account of Julia Roberts' whirlwind romance with Lyle Lovett, no one was the wiser. And when you were done, you placed the *Time* or *People* on top of the *Playboy*. Like I said, it wasn't an airtight system, but this was a barbershop, not the 1990s Chicago Bulls' triangle offense.

Unfortunately, Ed and Rich got older, and around the turn of the century, they sold Rialto's. When I found out, it felt like a punch in the stomach, and I took it personally. "How could Ed and Rich do this to me?!," I wondered, selfishly forgetting that Ed and Rich were pushing 70 and time was not on their side. Then, to add insult to injury, they sold the business to a woman, and I had never gotten my hair cut by a woman before. And that could only mean two things: there were no more *Playboys* and I wasn't going to the new Rialto's. I was a lost sheep in search of my flock.

I searched far and wide for a new barber, but none could cut my hair like Ed and Rich. There was one guy, Anthony at Continental Barbers, who liked to mess with me when he cut my hair. He would give me a normal haircut but leave a rat-tail in the back. There are just certain things you don't joke about, and giving me a rat-tail is pretty high on that list. So that was the end of Continental Barbers.

In the years since, I have overcome my fear of women cutting my hair and I have frequently strayed from the traditional barbershop with the candy-striped pole outside. Instead, I have been known to settle for the Burger King of the hair-cutting industry: Super Cuts. I am not proud of myself, but years later I am still shaken by the changing of the guard at Rialto's.

Alas, I do not have a rapport with the women of Super Cuts like I did with Ed and Rich. When I enter this gender-neutral establishment, it is strictly business. Well, sort of. When I check in, I give the lady at the counter fake names like Pedro. I always get a kick out of the reaction I get when I tell people my name is Pedro as they try to figure out if a guy with blue eyes, blonde hair, a pale complexion, and no mustache or sombrero could possibly be Latino. And when I'm done humoring myself, I'll often sit down, pick up a copy of *Parents* or whatever non-scintillating reading material Super Cuts has to offer and ponder why the prefix "uni" makes everything so lame. Cases in point: unicycle, unitard, unicorn, unibrow, and unisex businesses like Super Cuts.

In the absence of a personal connection with those charged with cutting my hair at Super Cuts, I do not know their likes and dislikes, or what they do for fun in their free time. Thus, when I do go back to Super Cuts and ask for The Anton Chigurh, I may have to explain that Anton Chigurh is the character played to critical acclaim by Javier Bardem in the 2007 movie *No Country for Old Men*, and I may have to bring a picture of Mr. Chigurh with me for visual confirmation. But that's no problem because I carry one in my wallet and because I am willing to go the extra mile to create some final fond memories with my remaining hair. I don't know if The Anton Chigurh is going to take off like The Rachel, sported by Jennifer Aniston on *Friends*, but a man without a little gamble in him isn't worth a damn.

To naked and untrained eyes, Turney Hall is not balding. But what they don't know could fill a book. I may sometimes unnecessarily refer to myself in the third person, but that does not mean that I am imagining my hair loss. Baldness is a journey that may include several stages of hair loss. For some, like me, that journey is a marathon, not a sprint, and it may take several months or years to show more obvious signs of baldness. *I* know that the end is approaching, that the days of my hair dancing in the wind as I

An Eagle Soars

frolic in the hills of New Jersey are dwindling. So when Candi at Super Cuts tells Pedro he's next, all chips are in, and I am going for The Anton Chigurh while I can still pull it off. After that, this eagle shall soar on his journey to baldness.

The Journey Begins

October 18, 1999. That is a date that will live in personal infamy. That is the day I found out my journey to baldness had begun. I was in the middle of a dream in which I had just set the world record for fastest backwards runner at the 2000 Summer Olympics in Sydney. Needless to say, the endorsements and the girls were rolling in. The phone started ringing, and I'm pretty sure it was Diane Lane on the other end looking for a date to the Oscars. Unfortunately, I never got the chance to RSVP because my alarm went off.

It was 11:30 a.m. on a Monday, and that could only mean one thing: time to get up. As they say, the early bird catches the worm. The day started off like any other: I did a few jumping jacks to chop down the morning wood, saluted the Andre Agassi poster on my wall, grabbed my towel, and headed for the shower.

Take a walk with me down memory lane as I set the stage for the day that will live in personal infamy. In the fall of 1999, I was a junior in college. I was average to below average in the classroom, more concerned with Sega than Sartre. You see, I had taken a shine to the amphetamine *Adderall*, which is used to treat attention deficit disorder. I don't think I had ADD, but my doctor was convinced that I did. "Do you ever have trouble concentrating?," the doctor asked during the initial consultation. "Oh, yes, doctor. I remember one day I was sitting in Anthropology class and the professor started talking about the Yanomamo tribe of South America. I really tried to lock in to the lecture, but before I knew it the bell rang, my Trapper Keeper was full of doodles, and I knew nothing about the Yanomamo." While the real reason I zoned out was because it felt more like *Yawn*-omamo and I would have rather been picking up spares at the bowling alley, the doctor opined that I was a textbook case of ADD and wrote me a prescription for *Adderall*. That plan backfired as the *Adderall* caused me to lose 40 pounds that didn't need to be lost on a 6'3", 190-pound frame, and to concentrate on the wrong things. So instead of hitting the books and making the grade, I focused on video games and New York Times crossword puzzles and walked away from junior year with a 1.6 GPA and a trip to summer school.

When I wasn't busy wasting my parents' money and actually graced the classroom with my presence, I needed a way to get there. And that way was usually my gold 1977 Lincoln Versailles that I had bought for $5 earlier in the year.

As ridiculous as it looked, I loved that car. It had 12,000 miles when I got it in 1999. A twenty-two-year-old car with 12,000 miles on it? Funny you should ask. Well, an old lady with dementia owned it before me--I mean, how do you think I got a running car for $5?--and her driving excursions were limited to the grocery store and the post office. Sounds like a pretty boring existence, but if you ask me, the less time old people are on the road, the better.

But the mileage wasn't the only perk--far from it. In keeping with the French theme, the Versailles also boasted a *Cartier* clock. It didn't work, but it gave me a lot of street cred nonetheless. The Versailles also had cruise control, an 8-track player, bench seats made of the finest pleather east of the Delaware River, and a steering wheel that did all the work for me. With the Versailles, when I was at 10 and 2 and smoking a cigarette, everything else fell into place.

Unless I didn't have money for gas. In that case, I would have to dock the Versailles until my parents deposited my unearned allowance in the bank or I could find enough loose change in the cracks of my sofa. If I blew my allowance too quickly on late night fortune readings from Miss Cleo or a new pair of Chuck Taylor All-Stars, I was never above inviting people to hang out just so the supply of spare change in the sofa could be replenished. My friends would think they were coming over to play video games or exchange lies about how many girls we slept with, but I had other ideas.

Unfortunately, most of my friends were as perpetually broke as I was and the sofa only had stale Dorito chips and lint to offer me on the day that will live in personal infamy. My back up ride was a Huffy dirt bike, but it had a flat. And besides, have you ever tried to ride up a hill in khakis and a pack-a-day Camel habit on a one-speed?! So I called on Plan C, a buddy of mine named Mark. As you can see, my friendships are typically one-sided.

Not including Mark, I lived with three other guys during my junior year of college. When our one-year lease started, half of us were losing our hair, and that half did not include me. I would regularly notice random hairs on the sink, in the shower drain, and on bars of soap. I felt sorry for those sons of guns: 21 years old and their whole lives ahead of them. But as fate would have it, the hair fairy decided to pay them an early visit. How could they go on? How?!

Thus, in 1999 I was aware of the premature baldness epidemic, but never thought that it would count me as one of its victims. So when I was hanging out with my roommates during the first couple months of the lease, I would often run my hands through my hair or put it in a vertical ponytail like Pebbles from *The Flintstones* just to taunt them.

I keep things short and sweet in the shower, and my routine was no different in 1999. Shampoo. Shave. Rinse. Conditioner. Full-body soap-down. Rinse. I am then ready to greet the day, and the day is ready to greet me. I'm no conservationist, but there is usually no legitimate reason to spend more than 10 minutes in the shower-unless you just came inside from making naked snow angels in Maine or you find out that you are going bald. And unfortunately for me, I was in southern Virginia and there was no snow on the ground. So, by process of elimination, you can understand why I spent 20 minutes in the shower on October 18, 1999, and part of the reason why that is a date that will live in personal infamy.

I was an *Herbal Essences* man in those days. As I massaged some Apple Blossom-scented shampoo in my hair, and contemplated cutting my 12:30 pm journalism class, I noticed my fingers were wrapped with several dirty blonde hairs. At first I figured some of the hairs that my roommates left on the *Zest* bar or in the shower drain had somehow transferred to my fingers. However, I was quick to remember that one of my balding roommates had red hair, and the other black, and upon closer inspection I saw that the hairs between my fingers were neither red nor black. Taken aback, I decided to run a test and continued with my routine by applying some conditioner to my hair. And sure enough, when I performed the next rinse, there were more dirty blonde hairs woven between my fingers. This had never happened before. What was on my dirty blonde head, stayed on my dirty blonde head. As my life flashed before my eyes, I could not understand what was transpiring. Could it be? Could there now be three-quarters of my house losing their hair? Is it the *Adderall* that is causing my hair to drop as quickly as my GPA? Would girls ever give me the time of day again?

As I wiped the tears from my eyes and waived my fists in the air, I could think of only two things that could help ease the pain: a rerun of the sitcom *Wings* on the USA Network and bong hits. The phrase "give that man a raise" couldn't have applied more to whoever was in charge of casting, because Tim Daly's straight man and Steven Weber's ne'er-do-well younger brother were comic gold as Nantucket pilots and the perfect tonic for a young man who just found out he is going bald.

As the end credits rolled, I heard a knock on the door. It was Mark. Now, Mark and I had shared many secrets during our friendship--like how if I had a time machine my first stop would be 1968 so I could put on a turtleneck and cuddle with Raquel Welch-- but as he knocked that day I was not prepared to tell him that I had just found out I was going bald or that I was a closet *Wings* fan. I had a reputation to uphold. Not a great one, but a reputation that did not include baldness or lame sitcoms.

When I invited Mark inside, he noticed the bong sitting on my table and his eyes lit up like a tweener at a Taylor Swift concert. We had a few minutes to kill before our journalism class, and we figured this was time better spent than discussing the day's reading assignment. We were now ready to learn.

It was about a ten-minute ride from my house to campus. Or about nine minutes too long. Mark is from Jackson, Mississippi and his love of Jefferson Davis was matched only by his love of Toby Keith. And, as if to prove how dedicated he was to Toby Keith, the CD player in Mark's pick up truck was always loaded with his music and he would sing along to convince the world he knew all of the words to his songs. I suppose it's a small price to pay for a free ride.

As we rolled up to campus, we found a parking spot none too far from the classroom. We were near the freshman dorms and the cafeteria, so there was a steady flow of students crossing the street to get to and from class. We were both feeling a bit lightheaded, and debated whether we should take the plunge and actually show up for class. I voted "yea," whereas Mark was a resounding "nay." Like a groom who got cold feet five minutes before his wedding, Mark wasn't sure he could muster up the courage to go to class in his current state. However, I decided to dabble in the art of persuasion and I presented my case for going to class: a check mark on the attendance sheet, Jill Merritt sits in the front row, and a little knowledge to boot. "Well, knowledge *is* power, and Jill *is* pretty hot, so I guess I'll change my nay to a yea," Mark replied.

To class we went. However, as we were floating down the sidewalk, we saw a red Mazda Miata racing down the street. As I remembered the bumper sticker I once saw on I-95 -- *I'm not gay, but my Miata is* -- and giggled, I noticed a female student crossing the street ahead of the oncoming Miata. I wasn't at my mental peak, but I remembered a few things I learned in my sophomore physics and Spanish classes and figured that a Miata headed at an accelerated speed toward a human being no es bueno. Before the Miata reached the girl, the driver was able to put on the brakes. However, he could not avoid a collision, and the girl, who was probably thinking how she would have preferred a more legitimate car to cause her demise, rolled up the hood and fell to the pavement as her textbooks flew in the air. I thought she was dead, Mark thought she was dead, but somehow, someway, she miraculously sprang to her feet and dusted herself off.

As the twenty or so of us onlookers stood there paralyzed with our hands on our faces like Macaulay Culkin in *Home Alone*, a European-looking man in a Magic 8-ball jacket exited the Miata to make sure there were no marks on his car...*and then* checked if his victim was all right. I imagine the 8-ball on the back of his jacket told him "outlook good," because he got back in his Miata and carried on his way- most likely to a *Wham!* reunion concert.

Glad to see the girl was okay, Mark and I were certain that someone was going to call the cops, and the last thing we wanted to do was give an eyewitness statement to the police. There were enough witnesses in the crowd--people who could give a more coherent account of the accident. So like any Good Samaritan, we exited stage right and picked up the pace to class.

When we approached the front door of the classroom building, I told myself that when my prescription windshield business finally took off and people would no longer have to wear glasses or contacts when they drive, I would become a philanthropist, donate a bunch of money for a new building and have the college name it "Hall Hall." Despite my choice in exercising the naming rights to the building, I figured that my school would still appreciate that gift more than when a few months prior I proudly donated to the library my copy of *"High and Tight: The Rise and Fall of Dwight Gooden and Darryl Strawberry."*

As I brought my head down from the clouds, and pulled on the door to the building, Mark grabbed my arm and told me he couldn't do it. The paranoia was too much for him, and my persuasion skills would be of no further use. I would now have to go on this mission alone. I just didn't know at the time that it would be a Kamikaze mission.

Professor Jensen started every class by taking attendance and asking anyone if he or she had a story to share. Nobody ever bit, because we either led really uneventful lives or because any story we could think of was inappropriate for the classroom. But lucky for the class, and unlucky for me, my right hand shot up in the air like it had overpowered my common sense in a no-holds-barred death match. "Mr. Hall, what do you have for us today," Professor Jensen asked curiously. "I saw a girl get hit by a car and I found out I am going bald," I said as I suddenly realized what words had left my mouth and wished I could jump out of the second story window without breaking an ankle or getting grass stains on my khakis.

Not surprisingly, I sat in the back row that day. The entire class craned their necks to face me and I heard a few exclamations of "What?!" and "Oh, my God!" I wasn't sure if the gasps were in reaction to the girl getting hit by the car or to me going bald, or both, but I was sure that I wished Mark had been there so I could have passed the buck to him.

I am not a fan of the spotlight, and the marijuana failed to magically turn me into Senator Chuck Schumer of New York (as they say, Senator Schumer loves the camera so much that the most dangerous place in America is between him and a camera). From what I can remember from that fateful day, all I could get out were a couple "ers" and "ums" and "it was awful" as the sweat poured down my face and my butt cheeks clenched. The class wanted more, but Professor Jensen knew I was in no state to please the crowd, so he pulled the plug on story time. Needless to say, the rest of the class hour felt like two weeks and there was no chance Jill Merritt would be attending Homecoming with me. Like Daniel Day Lewis and *My Left Foot*, it was Turney Hall and *My Right Hand*. Why did I have to raise it? Why?!

When the bell finally rang, I managed to walk out of the class with a few laughs and pats on the back. Again, I wasn't entirely sure if the laughs and pats were due to my failed story or because everyone in class now knew I was going bald. However, I did know that I should have listened to Nancy Reagan when she told me to just say no; that it can't be fun to get hit by a car; and that October 18, 1999, would be a date that would live in personal infamy.

The Epiphany

Crime doesn't pay. However, let's suppose that one day, perhaps a Sunday in July, I forget those words of wisdom. I am taking a leisurely walk down the Mall in our nation's capital, Washington D.C. I notice a gentleman in jean shorts, white socks and sandals, and a Jeff Gordon #24 t-shirt sitting on a bench near the Lincoln Memorial. As I debate whether I fear more the rise of Islamic fundamentalism or the rise of NASCAR, I see that wrapped snuggly around this gentleman's waist is a red, white, and blue fanny pack.

I ask this gentleman where he got his fanny pack. He tells me that he bought it from a street vendor about twenty blocks away. As he explains to me how to find this vendor, I can barely contain myself as I imagine the limitless storage possibilities this fanny pack could offer me. Wallet? Check. Cell phone? Check. Hacky sack? *Double* check. I would no longer need to wear pants with pockets- I could wear sweatpants morning, noon, and night. Besides, that's the direction in which the American workplace dress code is headed anyway.

As I envision my life without pockets, I also think to myself that there's nothing leisurely about a twenty-block walk through the nation's capital in July. I need a more convenient mode of transportation than my sneakers could provide. I reach into my pockets- perhaps for the last time- and I realize that I only have a $5 bill. On the plus side, the fanny pack I desire is $4.99; on the down side, the lowly penny is nowhere near enough money for cab, bus,

An Eagle Soars

or Metro fare, or enough to convince a bum to give me a piggy-back ride. Alas, I need another plan.

I scour the Mall and, to my surprise, I notice a *Segway* left unattended under a cherry blossom tree about thirty yards away. Desperate for the red, white, and blue pack of patriotism, I suffer a momentary lapse in judgment, and during this lapse in judgment I not only forget that crime doesn't pay, I also forget half of the adage that *Segways* and prostitutes are fun to ride but you don't want anyone to see you riding them.

As the owner of the *Segway* takes advantage of a photo op, I make my move and swipe the biggest consumer bust since green Heinz ketchup. I escape unnoticed--or so I think. Unbeknownst to me, there are several witnesses--including a beautiful woman in her 20s--who see me as I *Segway* from the scene of the crime. The police are promptly summoned and they bring a sketch artist with them.

Now, in one scenario, I have a full head of hair. A policeman questions the beautiful young woman and she describes the suspect (me) with stunning detail and accuracy. As the sketch artist puts pencil to pad, the witness states:

> He is really good looking, officer. I mean, this guy has a Hollywood face. I don't know if he acts or sings, or does both like Joey Lawrence, but he should because I would pay top dollar to stare at him for a couple of hours. He was about 6'3" and 240 lbs. He must work out, because as he was riding away, I think he flexed his muscles and a group of birds immediately scattered. Oh, and he had a thick, lustrous head of hair. I'm talking Leslie Nielsen thick. I would love to run my fingers through it all summer long, and probably the winter, too. If you catch

him officer, don't throw the book at him. I mean, his hair is just too full of life to rot in prison. *Owning* a *Segway-* that's the real crime. I hope this helps, officer. If you track down this Adonis, please give him my number. You know, in case he needs someone to post bail.

In the second scenario, my physical features are the same except instead of a full head of hair, I sport a few wisps of coverage in the front and a bare spot on the back of my head with the same circumference as a hockey puck. The police ask the same young woman to describe the suspect (me), and she immediately bursts into tears:

It was awful, officer. He was balding so badly. I couldn't get a good look at his face because his baldness paralyzed me with horror. I mean, as he was riding away I think I saw even more hair fall out of his head. You need to get *those* people off the streets, officer. The world is no longer a safe place, what with all these bald people running around being bald and committing crimes. Lock him up and throw away the key. Here is my number, officer. If you need me to pick him out of a lineup, I can be there lickety-split. I'd recognize his male pattern baldness anywhere. This bald animal needs to be caged.

These are the kind of scenarios that ran through my mind in the aftermath of the day that will live in personal infamy, October 16, 1999. And it didn't take me long to realize I would prefer scenario number one. However, it did take me a long time to act on it. I did not see a doctor about my hair loss until the fall of 2001, two years after it had begun. I attribute this delay to the first two stages of grief- denial and anger. For a while, I wanted to believe that my unexpected hair loss was due not to genetics, but to *Adderall*, because my hair loss began around the same time I began taking the prescription drug. Thus, the hair loss and the summer school experience provided the requisite incentive to part ways with *Adderall*. While overcoming legal speed was the right move, I was only kidding myself, because deep down I knew that the baldness bell tolled for me regardless of the *Adderall*.

And like the interstate family road trip in which the two kids are constantly fighting in the back seat and the mother is so fed up that she proclaims, "Fine. Kill each other. See if I care," I was so mad at my hair, as if it had the ability to reason, that I threw down the gauntlet and said "Fine. Fall out. See if I care." While kids generally stop the infighting after their mother makes such a bold statement, my hair called my bluff and continued to fall out.

I was 23 years old at the time of my first baldness consultation, and still under my parents' health plan. The family doctor, Dr. Garrison, was a fat man with a mustache and a full head of hair. As a rule, I do not trust men with mustaches. As I see it, a man with a mustache is hiding something other than his upper lip, and it may involve anything from a child porn addiction to a love of Renaissance fairs. Whatever it is, I don't want to find out, so I keep my interactions with mustachioed men to a minimum. As another rule, I do not trust fat doctors. It is difficult to take advice on healthy living from an M.D. with three chins and *Big Mac* sauce on his shirt. And yet another rule: I do not like to get tips on the treatment of hair loss from a middle-aged man with a lion's mane on top of his head. Thus, my trip to see Dr. Garrison flew in the face of several rules in my rule-book. However, there are exceptions to every rule – especially when your parents are footing the bill.

As I sat on the examination table, I explained my concerns to Dr. Garrison. "I'm a young man," I said. "I don't get all the girls, but I can guarantee you that if I lose the locks, it's going to be goodbye ladies, hello lonely nights. Help me, doc. Help me." As he slapped on latex gloves and examined my head with a flashlight, I clenched my fists and prepared myself for the worst.

"Ah, yes," said the fat, mustachioed doctor. "I see some

separation." Puzzled, I wondered to myself what "separation" means in the context of hair loss: Does it mean that my hair is like a married couple who spend some time away from each other before deciding whether to get back together or get a divorce? Was there a chance that the separated hair would someday reunite, or have they made a permanent split?

"It's nothing major, but you *are* in the early stages of male pattern baldness," Dr. Garrison said, confirming that my hair loss was unrelated to the *Adderall*, and that separation meant that my hair follicles would never be as closely knit as they once were. When the doctor delivered the news, I felt weak in the knees and lightheaded. I almost fainted, but as I sat there in a paper gown with flowers on it, I told myself to man-up and confront the situation. "So, what's the next step, doc?" "Well," he replied, "I am going to write you a prescription for *Propecia*. It's a hair loss drug that is in pill form. You take it once a day, every day. However, I've got to warn you that there are some side effects of a sexual nature. Here is a pamphlet that you should read to educate yourself about the pros and cons of *Propecia*."

While I did not need to hear the words "sexual nature" come out of the mouth of the fat, mustachioed doctor, I knew I had a homework assignment with important implications. Thus, when I returned home from the doctor's office, I wasted no time in gathering the information I needed to decide whether *Propecia* would be the right choice for me. I made myself a peanut butter and apricot jelly sandwich, shut the door to my bedroom, threw on some Notorious B.I.G. to set the mood, and put on my thinking cap. I unfolded the informational packet and got to reading. Sure enough, the doc was not pulling my leg when he warned me of the sexual side effects of *Propecia*. According to the pamphlet,

> In general use, the following side effects have been reported: allergic reactions including rash, itching, hives, and swelling of the lips and face; problems with ejaculation; breast tenderness and enlargement; and testicular pain. You should promptly report to your doctor any changes in your breasts such as

> lumps, pain, or nipple discharge. Tell your doctor about these or any other unusual side effects.
>
> A small number of men had sexual side effects, with each occurring in less than 2% of men. These include less desire for sex, difficulty in achieving an erection, and a decrease in the amount of semen. These side effects went away in men who stopped taking PROPECIA because of them.

Rash and itching? A day at the beach. But these are the buzzwords a young, virile man does not like to read: "problems with ejaculation; breast tenderness and enlargement; testicular pain; nipple discharge; difficulty in achieving an erection, and a decrease in the amount of semen." So what you're telling me, makers of *Propecia*, is that if I don't want to go bald I should use your product. However, if I use your product there is a chance my penis won't work, I will develop boobs, and stuff might come out of my newly developed boobs. Talk about a Catch-22: I want hair in order to have a chance with the ladies and avoid becoming a punch line, but to keep my hair I need to take a drug that might make me *one* of the ladies and the butt of a very different joke. Hmm....

It became a battle between vanity and virility, and vanity won by unanimous decision. The way I saw it, these unmanly side effects only occurred in a very small percentage of users, so I liked my odds. And besides, if Rush Limbaugh and Bill Parcells could handle a pair of man boobs, so could I.

After a few months passed since I started taking *Propecia* and I didn't grow boobs or suffer from any other undesirable side effects, I figured I could handle popping a pill once a day for the rest of my life.

The only drawback with *Propecia* is the price. Insurance companies generally do not cover *Propecia* because it is considered a cosmetic drug, and my first post-parental insurance coverage was no different. I worked a low-level job on Capitol Hill for a couple of years after college, and while there were perks like getting my favorite holiday off (Columbus Day), I got paid like I worked the late-night shift at Arby's. Thus, $70-$80 a month for a bottle of *Propecia* put a big dent in my paycheck. But I didn't mind. I just had to wean myself from my debilitating Lladro addiction and all those John Tesh concerts I went to. As long as the drug did its job and kept my hair from falling out, I could have been sweeping horse shit for a living while jamming to Tesh on my IPod and still have been happy.

I didn't give much thought to any other hair care product besides *Propecia*. I grew up watching Sy Sperling, the founder of the *Hair Club for Men*, tell me at 3 a.m. that "I am not only the president. I am also a client," as he was surrounded poolside by beautiful women and fast cars. But you've got to do a little better than paid models and Pontiac Fieros to convince me to join your club, Sy. And while hair plugs have become more aesthetically pleasing over the years, does anyone really think if you leave work bald one night and show up with a full head of hair the next morning that no one is going to be onto you?! Some men probably don't care, but I've worked in a few offices in my time and know from first-hand experience how brutal office politics can be. I mean, you make one innocent comment about how Robin Roberts deserved to be voted off *Dancing with the Stars*, and pretty soon you'll know why the staples are always missing from your stapler. So if you want to get hair plugs or knock Robin Roberts' dance moves, that's your choice. As for me, I've learned to keep my mouth shut and hair plugs off my head.

A man with hair plugs, or a "plugger," is not the life of the party. I am not friends with a plugger. For that matter, I do not want to be. I have had conversations with pluggers and not only did I feel really uncomfortable, I couldn't take them seriously. A plugger could be telling me that he found the cure for the common cold and was willing to sell me the patent for $1, but I wouldn't hear a word he was saying because all I would be able to do is stare at the plugs, think how ridiculous he looks, and hope that no good-looking women saw me associating with him. I couldn't think of a more counterproductive wingman than a plugger.

I also chose *Propecia* over *Rogaine*, the other FDA-approved hair loss product, because I would only need to take a pill once a morning, whereas *Rogaine* comes in foam or gel form, has a powerful odor, and requires twice daily applications. The message

Rogaine wants to convey is "Use it or lose it," but all I can think when I see a commercial with a balding man staring at himself in the mirror as he applies *Rogaine* to his head is how I don't want to be that guy. And not because he has a huge bald spot on the back of his head. Plucking my overgrown nose hair and eyebrows is trouble enough- I don't need to add another time-consuming element to my morning routine or to smell like cheap cologne. No, sir.

When I said the price of *Propecia* is the only drawback, I lied. I took *Propecia* for eight years, and I always dreaded my trips to the pharmacy to refill my prescription. Let me first say that I resent pharmacists because they make a lot of money to wear a white coat and put pills in a bottle. Plus, they stand a step above us like they're Wayne Newton singing "Danke Schoen" at the *Borgata*. Sure, most pharmacists are nice people, but I had a hard time shaking the feeling that they were judging my decision to take *Propecia*.

When I would go to pick up my prescription, I felt like a timid high school boy who goes to buy condoms for the first time: My palms would sweat, I would hope that the store was empty, that the person at the counter was not a female, and that I could get in and out of there as quickly as possible. The difference between the high-schooler and me is that the high-schooler is presumably going to have intercourse after the condom purchase. He shouldn't be intimidated; he should be walking tall and high-fiving everyone in sight.

My pharmacy of choice, CVS, is never empty and there is always some old, angry customer who holds up the pick-up line because of some insurance coverage complaint. And the pain of such a wait is exacerbated by having to listen to Celine Dion or Rihanna rain down from the speakers above, and my constant worries about the person behind me in line peeking over my shoulder like a 5th grader cheating on his spelling test as he tries to see what I have a prescription for. So when it was finally time for the *Propecia* showdown between the pharmacist and me, I would be in a pretty unpleasant state of mind. But I kept my thoughts to myself, because the pharmacist was in on my secret and he had the upper hand. One snide remark or dirty look from me, and all he had to do was get on the loudspeaker, interrupt Ms. Dion, and ask for a price check on *Propecia*. Thus, my lips remained sealed and we conducted our business transaction like gentlemen. However, the internal monologues were deafening:

Pharmacist: "*Propecia*?! You vain, insecure son-of-a-bitch! You know how many prescriptions I filled today for Lipitor and Atacand?! I save lives for a living, motherfucker. You want hair on your head? Go tell it to a cancer patient. Get out of my store before I throw you out!"

Me: "Don't judge me, wanna-be M.D. I may be vain, but you're going to be replaced by a robot or an Indian in five years. And don't you dare ask me if I want a flu shot!"

Despite the price of the pills and the anxiety-filled trips to the pharmacy, I persevered for many years. I am just another conceited man who had been reluctant to play the hand he's been dealt. However, I like to think that the thousands of dollars I spent on *Propecia* wasn't a case of throwing good money after bad. I don't know if I would have lost more hair if I had not taken *Propecia*, but I like to think that the drug at least helped stem my hair loss and bought me some time as I came to grips with reality.

I can be hypocritical with the best of them. I raise an eyebrow when I see someone use the urinal and exit without washing his hands, but I have been known to do the same when no one is around; I pshaw aloud whenever I see a man wearing a Speedo at the beach, but *goddamn*, I wish to myself that I, too, could be that snug and carefree in public; and I mock Ethan Hawke every chance I get at a cocktail party, even though I'm first in line at all of his movies. But on the issue of baldness I have finally decided to take a stand and reveal my true self.

I had an epiphany, and that's when my whole outlook changed. With the help of some imaginary friends, a dusty Bible, my father, and a fat lady, I have been able to overcome my fear of life as a bald man in order to reach the conclusion that my only hope for a happy existence is to accept my hair loss. And while I'm no hero, I will not rest until every last man who is losing his hair may also roam the streets without being ashamed; until the bald have all of the same rights and equalities (replace equalities with privileges?) as the non-bald; until every little boy goes to bed at night and dreams not of becoming an astronaut when he grows up, but a bald man. This much I vow.

But how can I fight the good fight if I take *Propecia* to avoid or delay being bald? I cannot. Besides, I'm a family man now, and my money is better spent on diapers and matching mink coats for my wife and me. Thus, I have decided to say goodbye to *Propecia* and hello to my fate. Top of the morning to you.

Dinner and Wisdom Are Served

    I like to eat. I prefer to unwind after work at a table for one at Red Lobster, but sometimes I enjoy the company of others. I once read an interview of Barbra Streisand in the New York Times in which she was asked which six people, living or dead, she'd like to have dinner with. If you know Babs, you know she never disappoints. Her answer included George Washington and Albert Einstein. Those are solid picks. Both men certainly made their marks on the world and would no doubt carry on a lively conversation. If you know Babs, you also know she always inspires. So I decided to have my own imaginary dinner party. You didn't ask, but I'm going to tell you anyway. So, here's whom I invited and why:

    My first invite was Abraham Lincoln- the man, the myth, the legend. Before dinner, Mr. President recounted his favorite story about the Revolutionary War hero, Ethan Allen, to me and the other guests. In the post-Revolutionary War era, Ethan Allen took a trip to England and stayed with some friends. During that trip, Ethan had occasion to use an outhouse (Apparently, war heroes poop just like the rest of us). When he finished and returned to the main house, his hosts were laughing and one gentleman asked Ethan what he thought of the picture of George Washington hanging above the commode. And, without missing a beat, Ethan replied, "It's great; nothing will make a Brit shit faster than the sight of George Washington."

An Eagle Soars

However, Mr. President had to excuse himself early because Mary Todd had gotten into the medicine cabinet again. Fortunately, I still had two other noteworthy guests with whom to enjoy a meal: Larry David, the co-creator of the sitcom, *Seinfeld,* and creator of the HBO sitcom, *Curb Your Enthusiasm,* and Andre Agassi, the former professional tennis player. Now, it was tough to hold court with these rich and famous types, but after Mr. Lincoln excused himself, I got the ball rolling with a question about squirrels. It went a little something like this: "First of all, let me apologize for my guest's rude exit. And I know what you're thinking, "This guy freed the slaves and saved the union, and that's the best story he's got?" Don't worry, that's the last time I invite him to dinner. But his story got me wondering. I see squirrels everywhere I go. But I've never seen squirrel shit or seen a squirrel take a shit. Do they shit? I know if they do it'd be tiny, but mouse shit is tiny and I've seen my fair share of that. Discuss."

I played the ensuing conversation out in my mind, but I didn't really get the responses I had hoped for. Andre told me that, "Image is everything. Even for squirrels," while Larry offered that, unlike pigeons, we have no deal with squirrels. Perhaps Abe would have had a better answer, but I didn't gather these men to talk squirrels- that was just an icebreaker. Instead, I extended an invite to Larry David and Andre Agassi to tackle a more important issue, because they belong to an exclusive group, the ranks of which I can only hope to one day join: successful and happy bald men. Time is running out, and I need all the information I can glean before it's too late. As legendary UCLA men's basketball coach John Wooden said, "To fail to prepare is to prepare to fail." I want to be a successful and happy bald man, and who better to teach me about bald success than Larry David and Andre Agassi?

Larry David

Larry David is a bald god. As the driving force behind two of the most critically acclaimed sitcoms in television history, Larry has been able to use *Seinfeld* and *Curb Your Enthusiasm* as platforms to express his views and feelings on baldness. At first blush, you could say that he has done bald men few favors, for the main conduits for his views on baldness- George Costanza on *Seinfeld* and a caricature of himself on *Curb Your Enthusiasm* (Fake Larry)-tend to feed the popular perception of the self-conscious bald man. *Seinfeld* and *Curb Your Enthusiasm* also do not spare jokes at the bald man's expense, thus encouraging the anti-bald movement. But that's all right--bald men should be able to laugh about their baldness and not care when the non-bald laugh at them because laughter is a great cure for many of society's ills and hair loss *is* funny. While George and Fake Larry make baldness a disproportionate concern in their lives, they have taught us that it is possible to be bald and still be able to get up in the morning and tie your shoes just like everyone else.

Larry David has used his fame to speak out about baldness in other forums. When he won an Emmy award for Outstanding Individual Achievement in Writing in a Comedy Series for the *Seinfeld* episode "The Contest" in 1993, Larry got to the podium to accept the award and said, "This is all well and good, but I'm still bald." Perhaps Larry felt he could not enjoy his success as a bald man as much as he could if he were a successful haired man, but most likely Larry was just trying to get a laugh out of the audience. And by doing so, he assured people that he would survive despite his baldness.

In another clever spin on baldness, Larry did a promotional ad for the charitable program, Stand Up to Cancer. In the ad, Larry bemoaned the idea that cancer patients who lose their hair as a result of chemotherapy are stealing the sympathy normally reserved for the naturally bald. The solution, according to Larry, was either for bald men to all get cancer or to help support finding a cure for cancer so that the naturally bald man could elicit the sympathy he rightly deserves. He voted for the latter. Any man who has made millions of dollars despite being bald, and who can pull off a joke about cancer and baldness in an effort to find a cure for cancer, is most certainly a man whose perspective on baldness should be eagerly sought. And that is why I reserved a seat at the imaginary dinner table for Larry David. Surely, he could aid me on my journey to baldness.

Andre Agassi

An Eagle Soars

Growing up, Andre Agassi was my hero. When we are young, we do a lot of questionable things, and my phase of dressing just like Andre Agassi is one of those things. In the late 1980s, Agassi played a match at a tournament near my home, and my dad got tickets. I didn't really know who Agassi was at the time, but I soon would and the hero worship would begin. During a break in the action, Agassi lofted tennis balls in the stands, and if you caught one you could come down to the court and try to return a serve from Agassi. I had pretty good hands, so I put them to use by pushing a younger kid out of the way and catching one of the balls.

I was 10 or 11 at the time, and I was naively convinced it would be no problem returning one of his serves. On his first serve, Agassi decided to get a rise out of the crowd and let it rip as fast and hard as he could. I saw something coming at me and it was yellow, but that's about all I knew as I swung wildly and missed the ball by about 5 seconds. The crowd roared with laughter, and I looked like I was about to cry. Agassi told me I could give it another try, but after the first serve I figured that I would stand no chance at putting the ball in play. However, to my surprise, Agassi wound up like he was going to let another one dart past me, but instead dinked a serve so lightly and slowly that I was actually able to put racquet to ball and get it over the net.

By letting me save face that day, Agassi earned himself a new devotee. And devoted I became. Every time I played tennis for the next year or two, I would dress exactly like Andre. I had the neon pink and black shirt, the same racquet, the same shoes, and even had the acid-washed jean shorts with the neon pink spandex underneath. I remember the first time I tried the shorts on and cried because my legs were too skinny for the spandex, which just dangled and hovered pathetically over my thighs. While I'm sure my parents were extremely embarrassed to see me dressed like that in public, I think it's in the parental contract to love your children no matter what.

Andre's brashness and rebellious image really struck a chord with me as I went through my own phase of brashness and rebellion. I so admired his protests against playing at Wimbledon because of the all-white dress code that I decided to protest playing at my parents' country club on the same grounds. When Agassi finally caved in and abided by the rules at the All England Club, I didn't think he was a sell out, and instead I cried along with him when he won at Wimbledon in 1992, his first Grand Slam win. As you can tell, I cried or was on the brink of crying a lot in those days. But the same went for Agassi, so I was only trying to be more like he was.

There will always be a place in my heart for Andre Agassi. His career was marked by highs and lows, but he didn't let his career fall short of expectations, as he won eight Grand Slam titles, and is one of only a few men to have won at least one Australian Open, U.S. Open, French Open, and Wimbledon. And he did it all while transforming from a young punk with a feathery mullet and a penchant for crystal meth to a gloriously bald father and philanthropist. And that is why I reserved a seat for Andre Agassi at the imaginary dinner table. Surely he, too, could aid me on my journey to baldness.

Imaginary Dinner is Served

Me: I hope you guys like your grilled cheese sandwiches a little browned.
Larry: Who doesn't?
Me: Before we get started, who wants a shot of tequila?
Larry: Patron?
Me: Montezuma.
Larry: Montezuma? Did you find it *under* the bottom shelf?
Agassi: Image is everything. But I guess Montezuma will do.
Agassi: To the host!
Larry: To the host!
Me: Thank you, thank you. So, gentlemen, as you know from the RSVP I sent you, the reason I have gathered you here tonight to enjoy some grilled cheese and tequila is because I am losing my hair and I'm a little down about it. You two have been there and done that, and managed to carry on with your lives. How'd you do it? How could you show your faces in public?
Larry: First of all, this grilled cheese is delicious. Compliments to the chef. You've really outdone yourself.
Me: Thank you. But the credit really goes to George Foreman.
Agassi: Is there provolone *and* goat cheese in here? Nice

touch. Well, as you might be able to tell from that picture of me that you have on your wall, I started to lose my hair at a young age. But with all of my endorsements and the screaming girls, I had to keep my mullet intact, and I was scared to death by the prospect of going bald in front of millions of people.

Me: I once paid a group of girls to scream and rip my shirt as I walked through a mall to make it look like I was famous. Onlookers were taking my picture even though they had no idea who I was. So I know what you mean, man.

Agassi: Anyway...if you pick up a copy of my autobiography, "Open," which is available in bookstores across the country and in Europe, too, you'll learn all about my struggles with baldness. I actually wore a hairpiece in the late eighties and early nineties, and I was terrified of what the world would think of me if they knew I was living a lie. I brought a copy of "Open" with me to dinner, so let me read you an excerpt to make a long story short.

Larry: Let me tell you something, Agassi. If you're going to tell us that you're going to make a long story short, it better be short or it better be good. I've heard too many people say, "I'm going to make a long story short," twenty minutes before the story is over.

Agassi: Got it. Let me set the stage by saying it was 1990, and I was playing in my first Grand Slam final at the French Open. When I wasn't hitting winners down the line, I was getting all the girls. By the Peugeot-load. Well, the night before the match, my hairpiece fell apart and I panicked. I was able to put it back together with bobby pins, but all I could think about during my match was my hairpiece falling off. On page 152, this is how I explained what was going through my mind:

> Of course I could play without my hairpiece. But after months and months of derision, criticism, mockery, I'm too self-conscious. *Image is Everything?* What would they say if they knew I've been wearing a hairpiece all this time? Win or lose, they wouldn't talk about my game. They would talk only about my hair.

I dodged a bullet when the hairpiece stayed put, but I lost the match.

Me: That was a hairpiece?! You had me fooled. Kudos. My parents thought you were gay, but I told them they were gay. You haven't been pulling my chain on that too, right?

Agassi: Straight as an arrow. Brooke Shields kind of looks like a man, but trust me, she's all woman.

Me: Phew.

Larry: You may have lied about your baldness, but you kept your word about making a long story short. Another shot?

Me and Agassi: Sure.

All: To baldness!

Larry: And to making long stories short!

Me: And to Agassi not being gay!

Me: So what changed, Andre? I mean, you got rid of the hairpiece-aided mullet at some point and bared your baldness by shaving your head.

Agassi: I had no choice. I took one look at the disarray that was Pete Sampras' balding head, and I knew what I had to do. I *had* to shave my head.

Me: Tee-hee.

Agassi: But seriously, if you buy a copy of my autobiography, "Open," you'll learn all about my decision to expose my baldness. But since you make one heck of a grilled cheese, I'm going to share another excerpt with you for free. It was actually Brooke who convinced me in the mid-1990s that it was time to let the public know for certain that I was going bald and we invited some friends over to witness the momentous occasion. So, turning to page 198 of my autobiography, "Open," which is available in bookstores, I said,

> As night turns to morning, as we work our way through several bottles of wine, I feel exhilarated, and heavily indebted to Brooke. You were right, I tell her. My hairpiece was a shackle, and my natural hair, grown to absurd lengths, dyed three different colors, was a weight as well,

holding me down. It seems so trivial -- hair. But hair has been the crux of my public image, and my self-image, and it's been a sham. Now the sham is lying on Brooke's floor in tiny haystacks. I feel well rid of it. I feel true. I feel free. And I play like it. At the 1995 Australian Open I come out like the Incredible Hulk. I don't drop one set in a take-no-prisoners blitz to the final.

It's my second slam in a row, my third overall. Everyone says it's my best slam yet, because it's my first victory over Pete in a slam final. But I think twenty years from now I'll remember it as my first bald slam.

Larry: I didn't realize it is open mike night.

Me (holding back tears): That's a beautiful story, man. You went bald, but you were still able to hit the tennis ball. That is truly inspiring.

Agassi: I know. And I was still able to get the girl of my dreams when I got divorced from Brooke Shields and married Steffi Graf.

Me: Wow. Dreams *do* come true. Does anyone have a tissue? I'm a sucker for happy endings.

Agassi: Here you go (handing me a tissue). Another shot?

Larry: Line them up, and allow me to add my two cents. I'll keep this short. So listen, and listen good.

Me: Do tell.

Larry: A few years back, "Somebody asked me what it is I'm most proud of. 'That's easy,' I beamed. 'It would have to be the way I've adjusted to baldness.' I'm a bald man who's out there. No toupees, no transplants, no hats, no beards. Just totally unvarnished, unabashed bald. One of an ever-increasing minority of bald men who have chosen to do nothing." (Sydney Morning Herald, June 3, 2000).

Larry (continuing): So heed the words that I say, and proudly adjust to baldness.

Me: Thanks, Larry. That's some good advice. And no offense, Larry, but you're not the most attractive guy out there, hair or no hair. A woman would have to get past your facial features before she'd worry about your hair.

Larry: No offense, but I'm worth a couple hundred million dollars. What do you have in the bank? $26?

Me: Touche. I respect your decision to opt for the status quo, but I also respect Agassi's decision to shave it all off. Either way, you both have shown me the light. When I first started to lose my hair, I thought my life was over. I wasn't thinking suicide, but I wanted to move to the mountains of West Virginia and hide. I would befriend bears and coyotes. "Surely, they wouldn't judge me for my hair," I thought. After talking to the two of you, I now realize how ridiculous it is to worry about losing my hair. It is all so clear. I shall remain a part of society and embrace my baldness just as you two have.

Agassi: Image is everything.

Larry: Even if you're going bald.

That imaginary dinner worked wonders on my self-image. They not only liked my grilled cheese sandwiches, they provided me with much needed wisdom on the proper path to baldness. Baldness is not easy. It makes some of us feel old, some of us feel like less of a man, and some of us feel like genetic rejects. Larry David is a bald man, but I think of him first as a funny and ludicrously rich man. Andre Agassi is a bald man, but I think of him first as a legendary tennis player and philanthropist who overcame some poor fashion choices. They succeeded in this anti-bald nation despite their baldness. I will do as they did and not let my hair define me. We all have our own ways of dealing with life's changes and difficulties. For me, it took an imaginary dinner to help me accept my fate and decide to soar like an eagle through the stages of baldness. What could be wrong with a grown man having an imaginary dinner?

A lot. Therefore, I will say that the imaginary dinner was not my only source for finding the strength to accept my baldness. I also tapped into other sources.

Baldness and the Bible

I am not a religious man, but I respect the Bible.

My respect for the Bible started in high school. I was a gentleman and a scholar at the beginning of my senior year. My grades were excellent, and I was at or near the top of my class. On the strength of my academic record, I applied early and was accepted to my first choice of colleges. Then I hit rock bottom. I became the poster child for the "senior slide": smoking in the boys room and general irreverence took precedence over class attendance and homework. I had been on pace to collect awards by the truckload at graduation. Unfortunately, I had to cancel the U-Haul reservation after my grades plummeted in English, French, Russian History, and Calculus. However, there was one class in which my grades remained excellent. And that was Theology. The Bible really spoke to me in those days.

I was raised as an Episcopalian and attended church on most Sundays growing up. However, church was more of a burden than a time to rejoice. I would often stare blankly into the distance as the rector delivered a sermon on loving thy neighbor or pull a disappearing act when it was time for Communion. That all changed when I took that Theology class my senior year and actually cracked open the Bible. I did not become a born-again or anything, but the Bible was the first book that I actually enjoyed reading. Despite my academic achievement in high school, I hated to read. I once rented the movie version of *The Scarlett Letter* instead of reading the book. That corner cutting backfired on me when I wrote an essay and mistakenly stated how society mistreated Demi Moore.[1]

I didn't cut any corners in my Theology class and read the Bible with enthusiasm. And my diligence paid off--I didn't walk away from high school graduation empty handed after all because I received the Theology award. I also gained some insight into all the hype about God and Jesus. I now only go to church on Christmas Eve and I still have an aversion to reading, but my respect for the Bible remains, albeit from a comfortable distance. And one thing I have learned is that the Bible is more than just a good story. The Bible provides people with answers. When someone suffers a loss, whether familial, financial, or otherwise, a person may turn to the Bible for comfort and strength. If it works for stand-up guys like Jim Bakker and Benny Hinn, why not me?

I was happy to learn that, after all these years, I still had my Bible from high school. I suppose a Bible is like the American flag-- there's really no good way to dispose of it. I mean, could you really bring yourself to toss one in the dumpster? If you have one at all, you have one for life. So I dusted off my first true literary love and turned its pages for comfort and strength about hair loss. And the Bible didn't disappoint, as I learned a thing or two about hair and baldness in olden times, and felt better about myself in the process.

My research first led me to Leviticus 13:40-41. According to those verses, God told Moses and Aaron, "If anyone loses the hair from his head, he is bald but he is clean. If he loses the hair from his forehead and temples, he has baldness of the forehead but he is clean." I was relieved to learn that there were bald men in the days of the Old Testament and that baldness was not necessarily one of God's ways of punishing man for his sins. I was also pleased to read that God thought bald men are clean. As they say, cleanliness is next to godliness. Unfortunately, as I read a little closer, I found out that God was just telling Moses and Aaron how to spot a leper.

---

[1] Ms. Moore played Hester Prynne in the movie adaption of the book by Nathaniel Hawthorne.

It's like God gave Moses and Aaron gaydar, but their powers only worked on people with skin diseases. So, God was not showering unconditional praise upon bald men. Instead, God seemed to say that a man who has lost his hair is bald, and that's not great, *but at least* he's not a leper. Regardless, I will settle for whatever compliments God deems befitting a bald man, and if God thinks bald men are better than lepers, that's good enough for me. I mean, a leper isn't necessarily a bad guy--he's just got bad skin. If God had said something to the effect of, "He has baldness, but he is not a pedophile," I would have to reassess my feelings. It would be reassuring that God thinks bald men are better than pedophiles, but that's not exactly a ringing endorsement for bald men.

My next stop was the New Testament and the Book of Kings. There I found Elisha, the successor to the immensely popular prophet Elijah, who got to go to heaven without having to die first. Well, Elisha was on his way to Bethel when a group of boys began to mock him, saying to him "Go away, baldhead! Go away, baldhead!" Kids say the darndest things--just ask Bill Cosby. However, they must have caught Elisha at a bad time, or he was really sensitive about his baldness, because he responded by cursing them in the name of God and before the boys could say another word "two she-bears came out of the woods and mauled forty-two of the boys."

When I was a kid and got a little wise, I had my mouth washed out with soap or had my *Nintendo* privileges suspended and that was the end of it. I guess the adage "boys will be boys" had yet to catch on in the time of Elisha. Thus, God decided the just punishment was to be mauled by she-bears. I don't know why God chose she-bears instead of he-bears, but perhaps those who mock the bald would be a little slower with the bald jokes if they read the Book of Kings. In any case, I was overcome by a strange sense of satisfaction as I pictured those boys getting mauled by she-bears. It felt as if God was not just a friend to Elisha, but to all baldheads.

As I continued my study of hair and baldness in the Bible, it was with mixed emotions that I read the story of Samson. Samson was a Nazarite, and the most famous one for that matter. The Nazarites were Jewish folk who had to take a vow in order "to separate themselves to the Lord" (Numbers 6:2) from the Canaanites. This vow comprised three parts: Nazarites could not drink alcohol; they could not see dead bodies; and they could not cut their hair. As for Samson, his hair empowered him with inhuman strength: He killed a lion with his bare hands and slayed 1,000 Philistines with a donkey's jawbone. These feats of strength filled my heart with envy and jealousy. "That's impressive, but I bet *I* could kill a lion with my bare hands *too* if I had a full head of hair," I thought, deluding myself as I cautiously combed my fingers through my male pattern baldness.

Samson also loved the ladies. However, he loved one, Delilah, a little too much. And that was his downfall. In an early example of the great lengths to which a man will go in order to woo a woman, Samson relented to Delilah's persistent pleas to learn the source of his strength. As Samson explained, "If my head were shaved, then my strength would leave me; I would become weak, and be like anyone else." (Judges 16:17). While I admire Samson's attempt to win over Delilah, he paid a big price for revealing his hair's power. Once his secret was out in the open, Delilah passed it on to the Philistines, who cut Samson's hair. Having thus lost his strength, the Philistines were able to gouge Samson's eyes out. I was no longer envious or jealous of Samson. But instead of gloating over the troubles of a haired man, I felt a degree of empathy for poor Samson. I mean, I once chugged a beer at a college party to impress Katie Harrison but threw it up on her shoes.

While I could empathize with Samson, I found a silver lining in his demise. As Samson explained, his strength would leave him if his head were shaved, and "he would become weak, and be like anyone else." At first I interpreted this as an insult. Did Samson just call bald people "weak?" But I took a deep breath, counted to ten, and gave Samson's words a second thought. Samson would only become weak if his head were *shaved*. He said nothing about his hair falling out naturally. Perhaps this was part of the deal with God. If Samson and the other Nazarites promised not to touch their hair, God would not let them go naturally bald. At any rate, I took comfort in knowing that Samson would not have lost his strength if he went *bald* bald. Many balding people lose confidence and inner strength as they lose more and more hair. If Samson had lost his strength because he had male pattern baldness, this outcome would have been a devastating blow to the baldness community.

The last biblical hair tale that I read involved Absalom, the son of King David. In the book of Samuel, Absalom's features were described as follows:

> Now in all Israel there was no one to be praised so much for his beauty as Absalom; from the sole of his foot to the crown of his head there was no blemish in him. When he cut the hair of his head (for at the end of every year he used to cut it; when it was heavy on him, he cut it), he weighed the hair of his head, two hundred shekels by the king's weight. (2 Samuel 14:25-26).

I hated Absalom already. I harkened back to a time when my barbers, Ed and Rich, would make comments about how much hair I had and would motion to their helper, a mentally-challenged man named Bobo, every five minutes to sweep up the hair that had been cut from my head so that little children wouldn't drown as they walked past my chair. I don't know how to convert shekels to pounds, but I bet I could have once given Absalom a run for his money.

However, like Samson, life was not all frankincense and myrrh for Absalom, despite his good looks and flowing locks. Like many sons before and after him, Absalom rebelled against his father. But unlike most sons who rebel, Absalom paid with his life. His father, King David, did not kill him, but when Absalom tried to take the throne, the Battle of Ephraim Wood ensued. During the battle, "Absalom was riding on his mule, and the mule went under the thick branches of a great oak. His head caught fast in the oak, and he was left hanging between heaven and earth, while the mule that was under him went on." (2 Samuel 18:9). As he dangled from the tree, Joab and his armor-bearers stabbed him to death.

The first question that came to my mind was, "Why was Absalom riding a mule?" I mean, a mule is like the *Geo Metro* of the animal kingdom: slow and embarrassing to ride. Second, given the slow speed at which a mule travels, couldn't Absalom have ducked? These revelations made my detestation of Absalom grow like the glorious hair on his head. However, like with Samson, it is difficult to kick a guy when he's down. As soon as his head got caught in the tree, I almost forgot why I hated Absalom. And then I remembered that I hated him because his hair weighed two hundred shekels--and that was just the part that he cut off. Thus, I could not help but smile when Absalom's hair led to his demise. Now, according to some, Absalom's whole head, and not just his hair, got caught in the tree. But just like the story of Richard Gere and the gerbil, people will believe what they want to believe, and in this case, I want to believe that he got stuck in the tree because his hair was just too awesome.

So, not only did I get a chance to relive my glory days by leafing through the Bible, I gained some invaluable insight into baldness. I learned that God may have favored certain people by bestowing them with handsome heads of hair, but a full head of hair does not guarantee happiness or success. Indeed, as the stories of Samson and Absalom illustrate, good hair may become more of a burden than a benefit. Also, God seemed to have a soft spot for the bald. He not only thought bald people were clean, He she-beared those who dared taunt the bald Elisha. From a Christian's perspective, or in my case, a Christmas Christian perspective, I do not believe there could be a better advocate for the bald than God. Thus, if baldness is all right with God, then it is all right with me.

A Family Affair

People always tell me, "I wish I could be you." I just have that effect. Sure, the book that is my life has a great cover. I have a perfect credit score, I have a beautiful wife and son, and I can snap a pencil in half with my bare hands. But, walk a mile in my shoes, or better yet, spend a day in my boxers, and then ask yourself if you still want to be me. But before you do, just remember that you shouldn't ask questions you don't want the answers to.

Oh, you're still here. I guess you didn't hear the one about how curiosity killed the cat. Yeah, I don't know what that means either. But, what I do know is that you should hug your kids a little tighter and tell your parents you love them more often, because what you're about to hear will make you really appreciate what you have. Or what you don't have.

Shit stains, poop problems, Hershey hangovers--choose whatever alliterative phrase to describe the indelible brown matter on my draws, I've got it. And it regularly puts my self-worth in doubt and tests the strength of my marriage every laundry day. Move over Harrison Ford, I'm starring in the sequel to What Lies Beneath.

So, you think I should wipe more? Funny, I don't remember addressing a "Dear Abby" letter to you. Besides, who do you think keeps Charmin in business, motherfucker?! Or do you need to look at those photos again? Yeah, the ones I posted on the Internet after another day at the office toilet with a pile of shit standing three inches above the water line. No, a horse didn't do that.

Some people inherit tiny breasts. They can get a boob job. Some people inherit a big nose. They can get a nose job. I inherited skid marks. That's right, skids run in the family. I got them from my father and one day I will pass them on to my son. If it keeps up, the family tartan will have to become a pair of blue Brooks Brothers' boxers with a strong hint of diarrhea brown. Alas, there is no surgery to erase skid marks.

You wouldn't laugh at a guy in a wheelchair. So, now that you know that I, too, have a handicap, and that my life isn't just champagne, limousines, and looking awesome in corduroys, save your laughs for *The League*. And, as I sit uncomfortably at my desk and walk the halls with a limp, be thankful for who you are. As hard as it gets, life goes on. Just ask Corky Thatcher. So, I'm a' be me, and you be you.

Skid marks weren't the only thing I inherited from my father. That's right, I can also thank him for helping to make possible my journey to baldness. If there had been a prenatal test in 1978 to determine if your child was going to be bald, I wonder if my parents would have given the green light to the obstetrician to abort me if they found out I was going to be a bald man. However, that would have been pretty hypocritical. I mean, my dad was already bald when I was born. I wouldn't have blamed my parents if they found out I was going to be a serial killer or a male figure skater, but I would have taken it personally if they had cut my life short because I am going to be bald.

My father's journey was considerably quicker than mine has been. For him, it was more like a jaunt. He was 19 when his hair began to fall out, and by his mid-to-late 20s it was all over. The way he tells it, he has just as much hair now as he did during his disco days in the 1970s. For most men in their 60s, they would love to have the same amount of hair as forty years ago. But, for my dad, it isn't such a sweet proposition because it meant that he had virtually none then, now, and every day in between.

I never met my paternal grandfather or great-grandfather. They died before I was born. But I've seen pictures. Scientists can debate which genes cause baldness and whether baldness is inherited from the mother or father's side, or both, but all I had to do was look at those black-and-white snapshots of my forefathers to know that the odds were not in my favor. I quickly noticed that not only did my father, grandfather, and great-grandfather not like to smile for the camera, they were all balding by the time they graduated from college. Turns out they all got an education that can't be taught in textbooks. Call it the school of hard knocks. Alas, I could not ask my grandfather or great-grandfather how they coped with their baldness, but I could ask my dad. So I did.

My father and I don't share many interests. I enjoy watching sports and jumping over Great Danes to impress women, while he enjoys watching cooking shows and knitting Christmas stockings. But we do have baldness in common. So I decided to interrupt him one evening as Rachel Ray taught him how to make glazed Cornish game hen, and ask for some fatherly advice on baldness. He really wanted to get the recipe, so I had to ask quickly. Though I felt rushed and slighted, I was able to get the answers for which I searched.

My father explained that he never felt depressed about losing his hair at such a young age:

> Why should I have? I didn't have a choice. We didn't have fancy FDA approvals in my day. There were only toupees and doll hair plugs like Joe Biden has. I had a roommate in law school that was also going bald and he wore a wig. Boy, did he look ridiculous. I took one look at him and decided that acceptance is my only option. But I never begrudged his choice to wear a man wig. I didn't want to be seen in public with him, but people should do whatever makes them feel better about themselves. Things turned out

> all right for him as he got married right after graduation. I don't know if his wife knew about his wig before they walked down the aisle, but they're still married, so either the cat's out of the bag or he married a blind woman with no feeling in her fingers. So, to answer your question, no, I never worried about losing my hair. I just accepted it, because it's not worth losing sleep over. There are a lot more important things to worry about. Now, see what you've done? You made me miss Rachel's secret ingredient.

It all started to make sense. As much as I love my hair, the imaginary dinner, the Bible, and my father all made me realize that there is no shame in going bald. The only shame is being ashamed of going bald. When I see an ugly woman I do not judge her, because she can't help the fact that she is ugly. She was born that way. She should be able to sleep at night knowing that there has to be an equally ugly dude out there who is willing to take a chance on her. Liza Minnelli could have told you that when she met David Gest. Just like an ugly woman, I have no real control over my hair loss. I can either accept my fate or plod miserably through life just because I don't have as much hair as I did when I was a younger man.

My father accepted his baldness, so why shouldn't I? He hasn't always given me the best advice, like when he encouraged me to go to law school and I listened, but on this subject I can safely follow in his footsteps. Even though he started to lose his hair at the tender age of 19, he took no measures to attempt to reverse or cover up his hair loss. There is something to be said for that, even though I can't say the same for myself. But I cannot dwell on the past. I must now look to the future and get comfortable as I watch my hair slowly drift off with the breeze or swirl into the shower drain, never to be seen again. In short, I must accept my baldness.

The Science of Baldness

As a child, I loved to go to the public library. I was far from the quintessential bookworm, seldom completing my summer reading list. But when a homework assignment called for some old-fashioned research on Henry VIII or Aaron Burr, I rose to the occasion. I knew the Dewey Decimal System so well the head librarian asked me to train her new assistant when I was 11. They called me the Dewey Decimal Kid, or DDK, for short.

A person could really get some reading done at the library in the 1980s and 1990s. The word most often used at the library in those days was "Shh," because etiquette and library rules dictated that the library was a haven of quietude and solitude.

But with the rise of technology and the decline of common courtesy, the public library has become more like a social-networking site than a stronghold of silence and scholarship. I don't think anyone actually reads books at public libraries anymore, choosing instead to take advantage of free Internet access and loudly download the latest music from Lady Gaga and Kanye West. And talking is now more than welcome at the public library as people carry on conversations about their failed job hunts or child's soccer game without a peep from the librarian. Alas, I don't believe I have heard the word "Shh" used at the public library since Bill Clinton's first term.

But the library still has books and other resources that are helpful and necessary for a man with a plan to write his own book. Thus, in the process of putting together a book on baldness, I took several trips to my local public library to see if the DDK still had his magic. I occasionally had to threaten boisterous teenage boys with a wedgie when they ignored my shushing, but figured that a grown man giving a teenage boy a wedgie might be frowned upon and require me to register as a sex offender. No matter, because it turns out the DDK still knows his way around the library, and I was able to collect the information I needed despite the cacophony that typically pollutes the once hallowed halls of the library. I wanted to get the skinny on such things as the causes of male pattern baldness, what segments of the population are most susceptible to the condition, and the process by which male pattern baldness preys on its victims. So, let me get a little serious on you as I report on what I learned. Just try not to fall asleep.

Male pattern baldness, or androgenetic alopecia, is the most common form of hair loss among men, affecting more than 35 million men in the United States. "Alopecia" means hair loss or baldness, and comes from the Latin for "fox mange." Fox mange is a severe skin condition that causes foxes to lose their hair after they have been infected by parasitic mites. A fox afflicted with mange will likely suffer immensely from skin irritation and dehydration, act abnormally, and will most likely die if the condition is not treated within four months. A human afflicted with androgenetic alopecia may act abnormally, but the condition is not known to produce dehydration or death. As a man with androgenetic alopecia, I do not appreciate the association with a diseased fox, but since I do not have any connections at Merriam-Webster's, there is not much I can do about it.

For us men who experience androgenetic alopecia, we may thank our hormones and our genes for our follicular state of affairs.[2] Androgens are steroid hormones that control and maintain male characteristics. While the exact molecular mechanisms involved in androgenetic alopecia are not known, scientific research suggests that testosterone produced after puberty is converted into dihydrotestosterone (DHT) by the enzyme 5-alpha-reductase.[3]

---

[2] El-Samahy M.H., et. al. Evaluation of androgen receptor gene as a candidate gene in female androgenetic alopecia. International Jour. of Derm. 2009, 48, 584-587.

[3] Soni, V.K. Androgenetic alopecia: A counterproductive outcome of the anabolic effect of androgens. Medical Hypotheses 73 (2009) 420-426.

Then, DHT attaches to androgen receptor sites at the base of hair follicles and cuts off the blood and oxygen supply to hair follicles genetically susceptible to male pattern baldness, causing them to progressively shrink until they are no longer capable of growing hair.[1]

The normal cycle for hair growth includes three stages: (1) the anagen stage, which is when the hair grows, lasts for 2 to 7 years; (2) the catagen transition stage, which is when the cells in the hair follicles die, lasts for two to three weeks; and, (3) the telogen resting phase, which is when the dead hair remains on the head but does not grow, lasts for a few months. Then hair falls out and the cycle begins anew. Thus, on a normal scalp, each hair grows for a few years, rests for a few months, falls out, and then new hair sprouts.

However, in male pattern baldness, the length of the anagen stage decreases with each cycle while the telogen stage is constant or prolonged. Since hair length is determined during the anagen phase, each new hair is shorter than in the previous cycle as subsequent anagen stages become quicker, and the proportion of telogen hair increases. This leads to thinner hair with every cycle. As the time between the telogen stage and the regrowth stage becomes longer, there is less hair on a person's head. So, the hair of men with androgenetic alopecia undergoes a miniaturization process, going from long, thick, and pigmented terminal hair to short, hypopigmented, peach fuzz-like hair, until finally, the anagen stage becomes so abbreviated that new hair fails to grow long enough to reach the surface of the skin, leaving a bald spot.

In a normal scalp, two to five hairs are contained in a single follicular pore; a decrease in the volume of hair may be detected when the number of the hairs per follicle decreases and is replaced by peach fuzz. Actual naked scalp appears when all of the hairs in the follicle have passed through the miniaturization process.[5]

---

[4] Ibid.

[5] Randall V.A. Androgens and hair growth. Dermatologic Therapy 21 (2008) 314-328; Stough D, et. al. Psychological Effect, Pathophysiology, and Management of Androgenetic Alopecia in Men. Mayo Clin Proc. October 2005; 80(10): 1316-1322; Kaufman K.D. Androgens and alopecia. Molecular and Cellular Endocrinology 198 (2002) 89-93; Otberg N, et. al., Androgenetic Alopecia. Endocrinol Metab Clin N Am 36 (2007) 379-398; Rathnayake D, Sinclair R. Male androgenetic alopecia. Expert Opin. Pharmacother. (2010) 11(8).

Indeed, by the time a man has become noticeably bald, he has already lost 50% of the hair on his head.

Before puberty, the average male has around 100,000 hairs on his scalp. Most men will experience some hair loss as they get older, but the amount of hair a man loses, and how quickly, may depend on several factors. A review of scientific studies of Caucasian males shows that an estimated 14% of pubescent boys between 15 and 17 years old shows signs of male pattern hair loss; 30% of men develops such hair loss by the age of 30; 50% of men do so by the age of 50; and male pattern hair loss affects about 80% of men by the age of 80.[6] Now, these numbers will mean different things to different people, but it is generally understood that male pattern hair loss can start at an early age, becomes more common with advancing age, and the rate at which the hair falls out varies from person to person.

To me, these numbers suggest that those affected 15 to 17 year olds are probably going to have to take their cousins to the prom. As for the 80% of octogenarians who have developed some degree of androgenetic alopecia, I say congratulations for not being dead. And, at that age, you probably have a lot more pressing health problems to worry about than the amount of hair on your head.

Growing up, I was always told--and believed--that male pattern baldness was inherited from the mother's side of the family. Studies have shown that the androgen receptor gene is found on the X chromosome, which a son inherits from his mother.[7] Thus, popular wisdom held, and still holds today, that you could predict if you were going to be a bald man by whether your mother's father is or was bald:

---

[6] Trancik RJ, Spindler JR, Rose S et al: Incidence of androgenetic alopecia in males 15-17 years of age. Poster presented at 3rd Intercontinental Meeting of the Hair Research Societies, June 13-15, 2001, Tokyo, Japan; Kabai P. Androgenic alopecia may have evolved to protect men from prostate cancer by increasing skin exposure to ultraviolet radiation. Medical Hypotheses (2008) 70, 1038-1040; Hamilton JB. Patterned loss of hair in man: types and incidence. Ann NY Acad Sci 53: 708-728 (1951); Rathnayake D, Sinclair R. Male androgenetic alopecia. Expert Opin. Pharmacother. (2010) 11(8):1295-1304.

[7] Rathnayake D, Sinclair R. Male androgenetic alopecia. Expert Opin. Pharmacother. (2010) 11(8):1295-1304.

One day you visit your maternal grandfather at the nursing home.

Bored of playing checkers and waiting for death, your grandfather is overcome with joy by your visit and eagerly welcomes you into his room.

"Hey Grandpa. Wanna wrestle?," you immediately ask.

"Well, my arthritis is acting up, but why not?," he replies.

You and your grandfather start grappling on the floor and you put him in a headlock so you can study the hair on his head.

"I can't breathe," your 90-year old, arthritic, grandfather exclaims.

"What's that, Grandpa? Speak up, I can't hear you," you say as you stall for more time to study his hair.

"Uncle! Uncle!," your grandfather shouts.

"Have you been taking your Alzheimer's medication, Grandpa? I'm your grandson, not your uncle," you deviously reply as you stall for a little more time to study his hair before you get the evidence you need and finally show mercy on your elder and release him from your pretextual death grip.

As your grandfather struggles to

> collect his breath, you ask him if the bald spot you noticed while you had him in a headlock just recently formed, and hope that, until five years ago, his hair was as thick as Delta Burke's thighs.
>
> Instead, he informs you that it's been there since he was in his 30s, and you faint. Luckily, you are at a nursing home, and there is a nurse close by to help you back to your feet.

Scientists have yet to pinpoint the exact gene or genes responsible for hair loss; however, most agree that male pattern baldness is a polygenic trait, and popular wisdom may be shifting from the belief that the condition is inherited solely from the mother's side of the family, and that certain responsible genes may come from the father's side as well.[8] For example, in one fairly recent study of 54 pairs of fathers and sons, nearly 82% of balding sons had fathers who were balding.[9] That study concluded that that percentage is higher than the number that could be expected from autosomal dominant inheritance--that is to say the mother's gift of an X chromosome--and that the Y chromosome from the father may be chipping in.[10]

And to those who say Caucasians do not know what it feels like to suffer from discrimination, I say check the statistics, and you will see that male pattern baldness hates whites more than any other race. Yes, male pattern baldness is a bigot.

Asian and black men have, at various points in America's

---

[8] Ellis, JA, Harrap S. The Genetics of Androgenetic Alopecia. Clinics in Dermatology (2001); 19:149-154.

[9] Ellis, JA. Genetic analysis of male pattern baldness and the 5∞-reductase genes, J Invest Dermatol. 1998 Jun;110(6):849-53.

[10] Ibid.

history, fallen victim to the evils of racism by white Americans. Thus, perhaps as punishment and retribution, the white man is more susceptible to balding than his ethnic counterparts. Men of Chinese and Japanese descent experience male pattern baldness at a less frequent rate than Caucasians, and if they do lose their hair, they develop the condition at later stages in their lives than do Caucasians. For instance, Japanese men are 1.4 times less likely to develop male pattern baldness in each decade of life than Caucasians. And black men are four times less likely to suffer from male pattern baldness than Caucasians.[11] Indeed, some studies have shown that 96% of male Caucasians suffer from male pattern baldness.[12] The prevalence of male pattern baldness among whites is not an intentional form of reparation for non-white ethnicities, but perhaps they can sit back and smile knowing that the white man is paying the piper known as male pattern baldness. We still dominate curling and croquet, but rest assured, my ethnic friends, that you've got us beat in the game of hair.

This should be no small comfort. For while male pattern baldness has yet to be proven to kill a man, studies have suggested that the condition may be related to certain serious health problems.[13] For instance, increased risks of prostate cancer and early-onset coronary artery disease have been linked to male pattern baldness, particularly baldness of the vertex, or the top of the head where a yarmulke would sit.[14] In addition, male pattern baldness has been associated with higher incidence of obesity, hypertension, and insulin-resistance.[15] So perhaps instead of sweeping ice with a broom and hitting colorful balls through wickets while sipping Long Island Iced Teas, the bald white man should engage in more rigorous physical activities to ward off any deleterious health conditions he may be more susceptible to.

---

[11] Otberg, N, Finner AM, Shapiro J. Androgenetic Alopecia. Endocrinol Metab Clin N Am 36 (2007) 379-398.

[12] Ibid.

[13] Ibid.

[14] Ibid.

[15] Ibid.

Whatever genes predispose white men to baldness to a greater degree than other races, those genes, in some form or fashion, determine when a man will start to lose his hair, the pattern his hair loss will take, and the rate at which and the extent to which he loses his hair. Of course, the sooner scientists figure out which genes cause male pattern baldness, and the molecular mechanisms involved, the sooner they can find a medical cure. I wish I could help them out, but I almost put myself to sleep writing about what scientists know about male pattern baldness at this point, and since I have yet to hit the lottery, they shouldn't expect any research funding from the DDK any time soon. Besides, I have already found a cure that doesn't cost any money: acceptance.

Baldness and the Law

The law is both friend and foe to the bald man. The importance of a man's hair in a legal sense is not a phenomenon of recent vintage. For instance, in the days of the Roman Empire, baldness was considered to be a deformity. Julius Caesar sought and was granted a legal dispensation from the Roman Senate to wear a laurel wreath every day to cover his balding head; other Romans could only do so on special occasions. Perhaps Caesar's self-consciousness about his baldness was the reason he cut off the hair of his enemies. I suppose he figured he would beat them and then make them join him in the ranks of the bald. Caesar also famously combed whatever hair was on his head forward, in addition to wearing a laurel wreath, in order to try to mask his baldness.

I doubt Caesar fooled anyone. I've seen "Rome" on HBO, so I'm pretty much an expert on Romans. And I can safely say that most Romans were probably on to his shenanigans. But not only does Caesar have a pretty delicious salad named after him, he also boasts an eponymous hair style that thrives to this day, as men across the world emulate Caesar by brushing the hair on their heads toward their foreheads in an attempt to maximize coverage. Say what you will about Caesar, his neurosis about his hair, and the stylistic legitimacy of his eponymous haircut, but a man who has a salad and a hairstyle named after him has done pretty well for himself.

More current examples of baldness and the law abound. Unfortunately, not everyone can be a Roman Emperor and get special treatment as a bald man. Instead, case law shows that attempts to use hair loss to one's advantage rarely succeed and bald

An Eagle Soars

men cannot typically rely on their baldness for help from the law. Nonetheless, hair has played an important role in certain cases. The following workplace dispute and suspect identification cases not only illuminate the law's treatment of baldness, but also sadly provide ample evidence that the court system is flooded with unnecessary lawsuits.

In <u>Rhodes v. DC Current, Inc.</u>, William Rhodes filed an age discrimination suit against his employer, DC Current. Mr. Rhodes worked as a machinery maintenance worker for the company from 1992 to 2006, when he quit his job at the age of 47. In 2002, Michael Mollencupp was promoted to plant manager and, as part of his duties, supervised Mr. Rhodes. Mr. Rhodes liked to talk to other workers as he serviced machinery, and this caught the attention of Mr. Mollencupp. However, his efforts to tame Mr. Rhodes' gift of gab caused problems between the two men. During one incident in 2004, Mr. Mollencupp called Mr. Rhodes a "bald-headed pussy." In another encounter later in the same month, Mr. Rhodes called Mr. Mollencupp a "faggot" after Mr. Mollencupp told him to stop talking to a co-worker. After these incidents, the president of the company intervened and told the two men to "shake hands, quit arguing and if you don't I'll fire both of you fuckers."

The president's motivational intervention failed to resolve matters, as two years later Mr. Rhodes alleged that Mr. Mollencupp challenged him to a fight by telling him "let's take it outside you old, bald-headed pussy." Mr. Rhodes complained to the president that such aged-based discrimination was damaging to his health, and the president told him he should quit if his health couldn't withstand his differences with Mr. Mollencupp. Mr. Rhodes subsequently filed an aged-based discrimination suit against the company (federal law protects people over 40 from age-based discrimination), but the court found that he could not show that anyone discriminated against him on the basis of his age. And the bald insults hurled at him by his supervisor were of no consequence as the court found that "these occurrences over a 2-year period wouldn't have compelled a reasonable employee to resign." Thus, Mr. Rhodes was out of luck, and perhaps he really was a "bald-headed pussy," because it appears that Mr. Rhodes declined to accept Mr. Mollencupp's challenge to fight. I do not condone violence, but those are fighting words.

Across the Atlantic Ocean, a retired art teacher at a high school in Stirlingshire, England, claimed in 2008 that he had suffered disability discrimination by his students because they mocked him for being bald. The teacher, James Campbell, averred that his students viewed his baldness as a weakness and the resulting harassment impaired his ability to perform his job. A judge determined that baldness did not qualify as a disability under the Disability Discrimination Act (DDA), and thus Mr. Campbell did not have a meritorious claim under that act. According to the judge, "If baldness was to be regarded as an impairment then perhaps a physical feature such as a big nose, big ears or being smaller than average height might of themselves be regarded as an impairment under the DDA." Not only did Mr. Campbell lose his case, he gave bald people around the world a bad name with his antics. To claim that baldness is a weakness and adversely affects one's ability to perform one's job is a slap in the faces of the hard-working bald men who get up each day and muster the strength to contribute to society despite their lack of hair. With his lawsuit, Mr. Campbell set back the pro-bald cause many years.

While being bald won't usually provide a man with special protection under the law, another workplace discrimination case, Ries v. Croft Industries, shows that being bald can actually benefit a bald man in a legal sense. In that case, Jacqueline Ries, a Croft employee, claimed that she was discriminated against because she was a Baptist. As part of her claim, Ms. Ries stated that, "Mr. Bloomer, a former Croft employee, allegedly flipped his hair at plaintiff in an ungentlemanly-like manner." The court dismissed Ms. Ries' complaint because she failed to show that any of her allegations rose to religious discrimination. Mr. Bloomer presented a rock-solid defense to Ms. Ries' allegation regarding him. According to Mr. Bloomer, "I did not flip my hair toward Ms. Ries or any other employee working at Croft Industries, Inc., as alleged in Ms. Ries' Complaint and, in fact, am almost bald and have been nearly bald for several years." Thus, Mr. Bloomer could not have flipped his hair at Ms. Reis, because he didn't have any hair to flip. Case closed.

In addition to workplace discrimination cases, baldness has also been a central issue in questions of proper suspect identification. One of my favorite cases involved a bald man accused of a hit-and-run offense in Brooklyn, New York. In New York v. Krel, the judge opened his opinion with a succinct description of the issue before him: "This is a case of first impression presenting a novel inquiry as to whether a lineup of balding heads meets with due process requirements." As I read this case, I wondered whether the judge was reveling in his choice of professions as he wrote his decision. "The case of the bald lineup? Jackpot! *This* is why I became a judge. Where's my gavel? Let's light this candle!," he was probably saying to himself.

The defendant in the case, Yefim Krel, hit the open door of a car parked on the street and did not stop. However, the female owner of the vehicle with which Krel collided had the wherewithal to write down Krel's license plate number and give a description of the suspect from behind as he fled the scene. She told a detective that the suspect had "a bald spot in the back of his head" that was "distinctive." The detective was able to trace the license plate number to Krel. The detective asked him to come down to the precinct, and noticed that Krel was balding. The detective arranged a lineup with six men, all seated with their backs to the viewing window – to recreate the angle from which the woman would have seen the suspect as he drove away- and each with a certain level of male pattern baldness. It took the owner of the car only 10 seconds to pick Krel from the lineup of bald men. Krel objected to the lineup, arguing that it was overly suggestive and violated his due process rights. According to the defendant, "identifying someone from a lineup of bald spots is so tenuous, speculative, and inherently implausible that it is 'legally insufficient' to submit to a jury." The court disagreed.

According to the judge, "the bald spot of the defendant was the principal physical characteristic seen by the complainant during the crime. Thus, the police needed only insure that the defendant's bald spot did not set him apart from the others, i.e. that some other reasonably similar bald spots appeared in the lineup so that the complainant was not visibly oriented toward the defendant, and the court held that the lineup met this requirement. The case went before a jury, which found Krel guilty of leaving the scene of an accident without reporting property damage. While the fact that the woman caught Krel's license plate probably contributed the most to Krel's conviction, his "distinctive" bald spot helped cement the case against him. Krel thought he had committed the perfect crime, but his genetic predisposition to baldness assured that he would not escape the jaws of justice.

Baldness takes its toll on the police, too. In Boone v. City of Elizabeth, a man accused police officers of using excessive force when arresting him. On June 11, 2005, the police officers were patrolling an area known for drug activity in Elizabeth, NJ, when they noticed Bruce Boone holding money in his hand after engaging with another person. The officers chased Boone, who kicked down the door to a residence where he was finally apprehended. Boone's version of the events and the officers' version of the same diverged greatly. Boone argued that he did not resist arrest, while one of the officers, David Conrad, claimed that Boone resisted arrest and hit him; Boone stated that there were three officers at the scene, while Conrad said there were only two officers; and Conrad argued "vehemently that he is not bald, and that Boone has repeatedly described a bald officer with white hair above the ears."

Due to the differing accounts provided, the judge in the case submitted the matter to a jury. According to the judge, "On the issue of Conrad's baldness, Conrad points to Boone's description of one of the officers who apprehended him as bald...Conrad maintains that he is not bald...[I]n support of his contention, Conrad supplied the Court with a photocopy of a photograph that shows a balding, though not bald head. This Court finds that a jury will have to determine whether Conrad could have been described as bald on June 11, 2005, and to weigh the credibility of the evidence and testimony of the witnesses in order to determine what actually happened."

Whether Conrad took a few cheap shots at Boone or not, it is a little ridiculous that part of the case against Conrad hinged on a suspected drug dealer's description of the amount of hair on Conrad's head. Boone stated that one of the officers was "bald," but Conrad "vehemently" denied that he was bald, and submitted a picture of himself as proof. While there is a difference between bald and balding, to expect an accused drug dealer to know the difference, like he's a dermatologist, is a bit of a stretch. All he knew was that one of the officers appeared to have lost some hair. He may have thought that the amount of hair the officer had lost qualified him as a "bald" man when in fact a dermatologist (or a jury) would conclude that Conrad was merely "balding;" regardless, the point was that Boone noticed an officer who had lost some hair. This case illustrates how hair can play a crucial role in the legal system--and could mean the difference between acquittal and conviction under certain circumstances. That is the power of hair.

Take note bald men. These cases show that the law does not view baldness as a disability and that neither should you; that a man not only embarrasses himself and his family when he tries to claim that baldness is a disability, but he also brings shame to the entire baldness community; that a bald man should wear a hat if his hairline could implicate him in a crime; and that if anyone says to you, "let's take it outside you bald pussy," you better take it outside and show him who the real pussy is.

Looking for Love while Losing Your Hair

I sometimes wish we adopted certain traditions from other cultures. For instance, take castration and arranged marriage. Now castration never really caught fire in this country, but if American men became eunuchs at an early enough age, there would be no male pattern baldness in this country, and probably a lot less road rage and professional wrestling. As for arranged marriage, this tradition offers a more direct, if undemocratic, method of finding a companion than some of today's more popular alternatives. If a bald man were guaranteed a spouse without having to play the field, he would not have to worry if his lack of hair were holding him back from finding someone with whom to spend the rest of his life. However, until there is a less drastic medical cure for baldness than castration and unless arranged marriage becomes a common practice in this country, most of us are left to catch our own fish in the sea whether we are losing our hair or not.

When I ask couples how they met, I want to hear a good story. For instance, I went on a date with a woman during my second year of law school, and even though the relationship didn't last, I was so fascinated by our encounter that I couldn't wait to tell my diary the good news:

Dear Diary,

They say there's no place like home. I beg to differ. So, at the start of the school year I signed up for classes and went to work... scouting out the best place to take a shit on campus.

An Eagle Soars

Like a degenerate gambler on a four-day bender at the Mohegan Sun, I needed a system. Pen and paper in hand, I drew up the following criteria on which to base my choice: degree of privacy, cleanliness, ambience, and timeliness of toilet paper restocking. At last, in November, after disqualifying the library, cafeteria, and admissions office, I settled on the gymnasium since it rated the highest on the four aforementioned factors. If the gym bathroom were a restaurant, and I were Zagat's, it would get 30 points--the highest possible score. And while I am generally unabashed when it comes to number two, the gym nonetheless offers me an alibi. Once I enter through its doors, no one is the wiser as to whether I'm there to shoot threes or drop deuces.

There's only one glitch in my otherwise smooth-running operation. Each building on campus has a security guard on duty. So once you enter a building you must present a photo ID. No problem, right? Think again. I've been using the gym's facilities for two months now and the same security guard is on duty every day. Thus, while I no longer have to present my ID, I now have to make small-talk each time I come and go. Normally, we chat up the weather, politics, or Lindsay Lohan. But, you see, I generally don't like fraternizing with the employees of the establishments I grace with my presence. I prefer taking care of business and moving forward. However, no other bathroom on campus provides me with the comfort level of the gym bathroom.. Thus you can see my dilemma.

So today my stomach started to feel a little angry. I looked at my watch, and sure enough, it said 12:32 p.m.--right on schedule. To the gym I went. Today was my first trip to the gym in 2007 and the security guard, an African-American woman, and I began by exchanging New Year's pleasantries. I told her I expected big things this year and that I planned to come to the gym more often in 2K7. "I need to drop a few lbs," I said, laying down some hopefully hidden double entendre as I made an iron-pumping motion with my arms.

As I started to walk away, refocused on the task at hand, she replied, "You can drop a few pounds here anytime," pointing to her genitalia and laying a third entendre on me. Taken aback, I tried to stay cool, and responded with light, yet startled, laughter and picked up the pace to the men's room.

As I sat in the handicap stall, wondering what other surprises were in store for me in 2007 and enjoying the ample leg-room, I started to have second thoughts. She's pretty good looking, and in my 28 years I've never had an amorous adventure with a black woman. Why not now?

So I spent the rest of the session strategizing, drawing up the Xs and Os. The game plan I devised was to let the action come to me. However, if history is any guide, the "let the action come to me" plan rarely succeeds. Oh, how alone I feel sometimes, Diary.

She reminds me of Miss New York of VH1's The Flavor of Love fame, attitude included. And if you know me, Diary, you know I like a little 'tude in my diet. So after my chalk talk with myself, I zipped my fly, did a few jumping jacks in front of the mirror and headed for the exit.

As I approached the security guard's desk, I aimed to keep the conversation to a minimum so I could get home in time for CSI: Miami on A&E. "I really hope Lindsay gets the help she needs this time," I offered. "Enough about her, what about you?" she replied. "It appears the action has come to me," I thought to myself. Looking at my watch and remembering that it takes two to tango, I threw out something about cognac and fireplaces. The seconds started to feel like hours, when she exclaimed, "Say no more. Gimme them seven digies and a bottle of Courvosier."

Lucky for me, watching Yo! MTV Raps and The Ladies Man with Tim Meadows was finally starting to pay off. While I wanted to say that I have a cell phone, and my number is actually 11 digits, I knew the score. "Do you need a pen?" she asked. "No, thanks. I carry my own," I said with confidence.

To make a long story shorter, game on. For our first date, we're going to see Stomp the Yard. Her choice, but my treat. So, you see, Diary, home is where the heart is.

Sincerely,
Your pal Turney

To me, the circumstances leading to my connection with that security guard are a break from the ordinary, kind of like *Zima*.

Because if I were to take a survey on how couples met, I would be willing to bet the Season 2 DVD of *Diff'rent Strokes* that more than half of the stories I would hear would involve online services or a local bar. Not exactly edge-of-your-seat material.

They say "Don't knock it 'til you try it." That may apply to *Coffee Coolattas* from *Dunkin' Donuts* and driving a minivan, but it doesn't apply to online dating. I cringe when I listen to couples on *E-Harmony* commercials recount how they felt like they knew each other their whole lives the first time they met. That's great, but you met on a computer. There is nothing dynamic about that. It's cool to play solitaire or buy clothes on the computer, but the thought of using the computer to pay for a date reminds me a little bit too much of prostitution. And think of the children who may result from these online romances. Yes, the children.

I remember an old classmate of mine, Richie Travers. He was a test tube baby. When word of Richie's creation leaked on the playground, guess who had a see but no saw? Kids can be cruel, and I imagine their cruelty will not spare products of computer love: It's a bright sunny day and there are some children playing a game of tag during recess. Kid number one, Jimmy, whose parents were high school sweethearts, reaches to tag kid number two, Dominic, whose parents met through an online dating service, but misses. Jimmy is adamant that he applied the tag and that Dominic is "it," but Dominic refuses to be "it." Dominic calls Jimmy a liar. And in reply Jimmy tells Dominic, "Well, at least my parents didn't have to pay a computer to have me." Kids can be as cruel as they are clever.

Even though I like to knock online dating, I am not so obtuse that I cannot see the benefits it offers the bald man. Perhaps the bald man falls into a deep dating slump, and does not know where else to turn. From the comfort of his own home, the bald man can set up a profile on one of the online dating services. And if he so chooses, the bald man can set up this profile without any false pretenses. Thus, the bald man may upload a picture of himself in all of his bald glory; he may list among his likes, "Being bald;" he may list among his dislikes, "men who wear toupees;" and he may list as his role models Terry Bradshaw and Jack Welch. A vehicle such as online dating allows the bald man an opportunity to be true to himself and true to potential matches. Of course, the upside to such honesty is that any woman who chooses to match herself up with the honest bald man will know what she is getting into, hair-wise, and will presumably like the bald man for who he is. On the downside, the honest bald man may not get any matches. However, I commend the bald man who chooses to embrace his baldness.

While misrepresentation in any forum is frowned upon, no one should dial 911 if a bald man decides to play fast and loose with the truth by uploading a picture of himself from his pre-baldness days. The cunning bald man may actually have a trick up his sleeve: by pretending to be a fully-haired man he is just getting his foot in the door so that during a first encounter he can try to show his match that there is more to a man than the state of the hair on his head.

While I never put finger to mouse in order to find a date online, I should not cast aspersions on those who do so find a date. And I will counsel my offspring to take it easy on any classmates whose inception was facilitated by a computer. Because in the end, I want people to be happy, just as long as no one gets hurt and the happiness is not the result of any Philadelphia-based professional sports team winning a championship. I don't know how many of these romances result in marriage, but given the popularity of online love these days, it occurs to me that perhaps arranged marriage *is* a custom in this country. It has just taken on a new form.

Another popular place to meet women is a local bar. But if you've ever gone to a bar, or "the scene," looking for love or even a one-night stand, you know it is one of the most brutal and unforgiving places on earth. In baseball, a player with a .300 batting average makes an out in 70% of his at bats, but he is still considered a successful hitter. In the pick-up game, the same measure of success applies. A big reason for this low percentage is some dudes who have made lives harder for other dudes at bars. I am talking about the guys who drop cheesy pickup lines; who harass women when they want to be left alone; who prematurely ejaculate during a one-night stand; or who promise they'll call a girl after sleeping with her and then pull a disappearing act--*those* guys. On the flip side, there are dudes who are so good at picking up women at bars that they leave nothing but scraps for everybody else.

Over the years, I developed my own rules for surviving and thriving on "the scene:"

Proceed with caution when one-night standing with a chick with a boyfriend in, or recently released from, prison for murder.

Throw caution to the wind if he's in for embezzlement or tax evasion.

You know you're into a woman when you can picture her with her head shaved and still want to sleep with her.

Don't date women with more hair on their arms than you have.

A pair of glasses can turn an average looking woman into above average. Cases in point: Sarah Palin and Lisa Loeb.

If your name ends in "i" we have no future together, either one night or long-term. So, Brandi, Tammi, and Patti, if you see me out, turn around and walk the other way.

Never attempt to infiltrate a bachelorette party. You will get eaten alive. Even if you go for the weakest of the pack, the one who is desperate enough to give you a chance, the stronger members of the pack will close you out of the circle in a second unless you are willing to put on a cop uniform and strip for them.

When you've been drinking at a bar, there's a big difference between 10:30 pm ass and 2:30 am ass.

Those with male pattern baldness should feel free to subscribe to my bar principles, and should never compromise their own principles when it comes to "the scene." However, a man who is losing his hair may have to adjust his approach. He will not have all of his hair to provide him with the confidence necessary to successfully woo a woman. But he needs to act like he has a full head of hair. He must walk into a bar like he owns the place. But he will do well to remember that there is a fine and necessary line between confidence and cockiness. Nobody likes a showboat. Sure, the bald man could try to impress women by juggling tennis balls or hurdling a couple of bar stools without a running start, but there is a time and a place for such acts of wizardry. I don't know when or where, but not when you are trying to win over a woman at a bar.

I am no sexpert like Dr. Ruth Westheimer, but I can safely say that the ladies like a man who is comfortable in his own skin, who knows who he is, and does not dwell on his imperfections. The ladies also like a man who does not harp on their imperfections, but highlights their qualities. If you treat a woman right, she will treat you right in return. If she does not, she is not worth the time or effort. Same goes for a woman who only sees a man for the hair, or the lack thereof, on his head.

I often tried to mix alcohol and women at bars in my early twenties. The results of my chemistry experiment were themselves mixed. One time, I approached an attractive woman named Sally. Sally liked to talk. Sometimes I like to listen. It depends on how good looking a woman is and what she is talking about. Thus, the better looking a woman is, the more willing I am to listen to her talk about stuff I find uninteresting or abhorrent. After we exchanged names and handshakes, she immediately and eagerly began raving about her toy poodle, Foo Foo. Apparently Foo Foo was the cutest and most talented dog on the planet, and Sally tried to prove it to me by showing me a picture of Foo Foo in a pink sweater as she fetched the morning paper.

Although I played Ted to critical acclaim in a production of *Bill and Ted's Excellent Adventure* at Camp Sanborn when I was 12, I have no formal acting training. But in the old days, I could put on a pretty good show if it meant taking a woman home or getting her phone number. So even as I imagined saving a pit bull from the local pound to rip that pink sweater to shreds, I put my chin on my fist, smiled, and said "Awww" as she showed me the picture of Foo Foo. However, each time I tried to move the conversation in another direction, Sally would keep the focus on Foo Foo and bombard me with tales of their trips to the salon and the bubble baths they took together. After 45 minutes of toy poodle talk, I couldn't take it anymore, no matter how good looking she was, and I simply walked away before she had the chance to finish her story about the time Foo Foo got into the cookie jar and had diarrhea for two days.

That was a rare case of me rejecting a woman, but illustrates some of the pitfalls of meeting women at a bar. More common were cases of me playing the role of the rejected. It is no easy task merely mustering up the strength to approach a woman at a bar.

An Eagle Soars

First, I hate the way the system is set up. Tradition dictates that a man is supposed to approach a woman, and not the other way around. Thus, as I stated before, the "let-the-action-come-to-me" technique is not very effective. I mean, who do I think I am, a cool guy like Stephen Dorff?!

Second, if I came up with some topic to get the ball rolling, and invented some story about how I was a professional badminton player in order to spark some interest, my self-perceived wit often failed--more times than I would like to admit--to prevent a solitary walk home with my hands in my pockets as I kicked pebbles on the sidewalk. While I never had a drink thrown in my face, which according to the movies happens all the time, I received looks that I thought were only reserved for math homework or the smell of shit.

Of course, not all of the ladies turned their backs on me at the bar. I went to bars and was able to get non-working women to accompany me home. I'm not going to tell you what they looked like or whether I had to take a trip to the free clinic the next day, but I consider those to be productive nights. I'm just glad they weren't reproductive nights. Good times, but not the kind on which to build a life with someone. I never met someone at a bar who caused me to light up and say, "This is the one. There is no point to look any further, because I have found the love of my life. I can now die a happy man, but I don't want to die yet because I want to spend many years in the company of this woman."

Meeting women can be brutal, but there is hope for men with male pattern baldness. There is nothing inherently taboo or pathetic about meeting girls at bars. Unlike a *Star Trek* convention or a Long John Silver restaurant, a lot of normal people go to bars. Nonetheless, bald men should be able to look fondly on the moment they met their significant others and recount the story with pride. And that probably wouldn't happen if you met her online or at a bar. How would the story go? "As I caressed the mouse with my fingers, I knew that love was only one click away" or "I don't even remember leaving the bar, but sparks must have flown because the next thing I knew we were knocking boots."

While I can't force you to do anything unless you're in North

Korea and I take Kim Jong-un's job, I recommend that the bald men of the world go with confidence to where the women roam free and are not expecting, or fearing, to be approached by a man. But be vigilant, because unfortunately a ring on the finger next to the left pinky is not a guarantee that she is married. And that is frustrating. I don't know why single women wear rings on their left ring fingers. Is it just because they like as much bling as possible? Is it to keep guys from hitting on them? Prowling for women is hard enough without having to play such mind games.

Keep your eyes and ears open, men with male pattern baldness. When you see an attractive woman with a flat tire, pull over and assist her. When you see an unattractive woman with a flat tire, put your foot on the gas.

When you're at an airport terminal, choose your seat wisely. Do not race for the first open seat. No, no. Instead, stand in the background, find the best-looking girl adjacent to an open seat, and calmly assess the situation: Does she look like she could beat you in an arm wrestling match? Is she on vacation or a business trip? Is she a local or is she on a layover? Does she have a bitch face? If your quick inventory results in more green lights than red, change the status of your desired seat from vacant to occupied. In my opinion, it is better to sidle up next to a girl on vacation because not only is she more likely to be in a good mood, she is probably looking for all sorts of escapes from reality, and if you play your cards right, you can be that escape. And if you really play your cards right, you can become her reality too. All right, that sounds pretty creepy, but hopefully you catch my drift.

When you are at the grocery store, linger in the fruit section in the hopes that you can strike up a conversation with a woman who shares your love of peaches. Tell her that the best time to buy a peach in the Northeast is from June to August, and not to waste her money on any peaches before June or after August. She would be so grateful for the tip that she would insist on giving you her phone number. You would have a relationship built on peaches, and happiness ever after.

Male pattern baldness is not a jail sentence of life without parole in solitary confinement. Sure, there are a lot of women who are not attracted to bald men just because they are bald. But those same women probably have brachydactyly, have moles all over their backs, are horrible in bed, or have some other problem in addition to high-and-mightiness. So you're probably better off without them. But you could make an effort to show them that there is more than meets the eye when it comes to male pattern baldness and convert them to lovers of the bald. That is, if you don't mind brachydactyly, moles, or bad sex. If that's not your bag, there are plenty of women who are okay with male pattern baldness and are not surfing online dating sites or sipping appletinis at the bar. And remember, it works both ways. There are plenty of balding women out there who need to be wined and dined. Do unto others as you would have them do unto you and don't automatically disqualify a balding woman from your dating pool. You could just ask her to do the Sinead O'Connor thing and shave her head. Nothing compares to that.

I speak of my experience on "the scene" in the past tense, and offer unsolicited advice and opinions that I can no longer apply to my own life because I got married in 2011, I haven't had a drink in some time, and I am now a family man. Sorry, Stephanie Seymour. My wife and I didn't meet at a bar or on a dating website. And, lucky for me, she does not care that I am losing my hair.

I actually notified her of my one-way ticket to bald town on our first date. In my view, it's like if you have an STD--you should tell the one you're with. It's common decency. Besides, it would have been hard enough hiding all of my pornography and honorable mention trophies before she came over to my place without also having to worry if she were going to recoil in horror at the sight of an unusual amount of my hair in the sink. You know you have a keeper when your girlfriend stands by your side even as more and more of your hair falls out.

Her "c'est la vie" attitude toward baldness, and our shared interests in antiquing and Trivial Pursuit, convinced me she was the one. However, I still referred to her as my "girlfriend" throughout our engagement, because I could not bear to hear the word "fiancée" come out of my mouth. Don't get me wrong--I was glad that I was engaged to her. I just think "fiancée" is a really lame word. The only French terms I like are c'est la vie, au naturel, piece de resistance, double entendre, and ménage a trios. However, I had to quickly get the last one out of my vocabulary lest I no longer would have a fiancée and would have to go back to "the scene" or resort to online dating--or move to India and wait until my phone rings with a father on the other end with an enticing offer to arrange a marriage to his daughter.

The Grass is Always Greener

    What if I had alopecia universalis instead of androgenetic alopecia, and all the hair on my head fell out instead of a select few (or a select many)? While receiving an alopecia universalis diagnosis may be as disheartening as learning that you have androgenetic alopecia, there is a certain cleanliness and aesthetic beauty to alopecia universalis. Since all of the hair on your head permanently falls out if you suffer from alopecia universalis, you do not have to contend with unmanageable and unsightly wisps of hair as you do during certain stages of male pattern baldness. With alopecia universalis, you do not have to worry about bald spots, because your whole head is bald. With alopecia universalis you do not have to worry about an eventual horseshoe on top of your head, with only hair on the sides and back of your head, because your whole head is bald. However, every rose has its thorn, and alopecia universalis is no different. With alopecia universalis, not only is your whole head bald, your whole *body* is bald.

    When I was a teenager I could not wait until hair grew all over my body. I equated body hair with masculinity and adulthood, and I prayed for the day when I could break free from the chains of childhood and embrace the freedom of manhood. When I was thirteen and the first signs of peach fuzz developed on my face, I refused to pluck them off until my mom broke down in tears and my dad threatened to cut off my allowance. When my first pubic hairs sprouted out of nowhere like crocuses in the spring, I was over the moon. When I grew armpit hair, I knew I had arrived and would comb and blow-dry it like women do the hair on their heads.

An Eagle Soars

And when I grew chest hair, I voraciously volunteered to be on the skins team during pick-up basketball games, and once took my shirt off at a local KFC to impress some girls until the manager asked me to leave.

As an adult, I do not need hair on my body as proof of my manhood. Taxes, a slowed metabolism, and a bad back provide me with all the evidence I need. And there is a lot of hair I could do without. Allow me to explain.

While years of wearing knee-length dress socks to work and neglecting to treat my dry skin with lotion have left my lower legs virtually hairless, I do not rue those decisions. While people have commented on the lack of hair on my legs, there aren't many girls I know with leg hair fetishes, and there is now no hair to distract onlookers when I spontaneously flex my calf muscles at beach parties or the park. You're welcome.

My chest hair is not thick and does not provide full-coverage, so I do not feel the need to unbutton more than the top button when I wear an Oxford shirt in public. In addition, the extra pounds that I carry on my stomach and the ghost-white hue of my skin ensure that I now only volunteer for the shirts team during pick-up games.

My armpit hair helps battle underarm chafing and covers up the grotesque skin tags that have developed there, but I could take or leave my armpit hair, because I no longer have the urge to stare at it for hours at a time like I did when I was thirteen.

As for the hair on my face, I cannot grow a full beard, which in my book is the only acceptable form of facial hair, so the fact that hair grows on my face just adds more burdensome activities to my morning routine.

And I now shave my pubes for a more aerodynamic look and feel.

Then there is the hair that decided to grow a little later in life. I am talking about back hair, shoulder hair, nose hair, and ear hair. It's like there is an inverse relationship between the hair on my head and the hair on my back and shoulders. The more hair that falls out of my head, the more that grows on my back and shoulders. I have a theory that the hair that falls out of my head is reincarnated as back hair. Luckily, I have debunked the myth that if you shave the hair on your body it will only come back thicker. Thus, in the case of my back hair and shoulder hair, I shave with impunity and regularity. And I have to, because more back and shoulder hair seems to pop up by the day.

The nose hair has become a frustrating nuisance. I have a large nose and large nostrils, so people's attention is drawn naturally to my nose. Plus at 6'3", I am taller than the average person, so most people have a clear view of my nostrils when they look at me. Therefore, I have to dutifully trim the hair that grows out of my nose. I do not want to be known as the guy with hair sprawling from his nose like ivy on an East Coast university building.

My homeroom teacher in the sixth grade was Mr. Ripley-Mason. Aside from a hyphenated last name and other eccentricities, Mr. Ripley-Mason was notorious for his unruly nose hair. My classmates and I would actually start pools to wager how long his nose hair would get in a semester. He was a nice guy, but twenty years later, the first thing that pops in my mind when I think about Mr. Ripley-Mason is his nose hair. I do not want people to come to my funeral and say, "Man, that Turney had a lot of nose hair. At least now he can rest in peace."

I used to have an electric nose hair trimmer from The Sharper Image. It was one of my favorite gadgets, a notch below my electric toothbrush. The electric nose hair trimmer, or ENHT if you like not-easy-to-remember acronyms, would mow down my nose hair in a matter of seconds and leave me worry free and ready to confidently talk to shorter people. However, my ENHT broke a couple of years ago, and The Sharper Image went belly up. As a result, I am left with manual nose hair scissors, or MNHS. I know what you're thinking: "Poor guy." For a gadget analogy to illustrate the inferiority of the MNHS, the ENHT is like a touchtone phone while the MNHS is like a rotary phone: the MNHS can get the job done, but takes a lot more time and leads to more mistakes than the ENHT. I mean, have you ever tried to dial 911 on a rotary phone? If you have, you probably aren't reading this, because you are dead. That's what the MNHS is like.

The most disturbing bodily hair development is my ear hair. Ear hair is a classic symbol of old age, up there with an affinity for early bird specials and hiking your pants up to your chest. In my 30s, I am not old in the grand scheme of things, but when I went to get my hair cut at Super Cuts a couple of months ago, the woman who was cutting my hair took a razor to my ears. "What are you doing?," I asked, always on alert when getting my hair cut at Super Cuts. "Do I have ear hair?!" My hair-cutter tried to play it cool, and told me that it was nothing. But there was no downplaying the fact that I now have ear hair with which to contend, in addition to all of the other unwelcomed realities of aging.

A man with alopecia universalis has none of these bodily hair worries. He gets to live his life as smooth and shiny as an apple from a farmer's market in New Jersey. However, the thorn in the rose that is the alopecia universalis man's (alopecia universalist?) life is the lack of eyebrows. I'm sorry for my bluntness, but that ain't right. I liken alopecia universalis to when you go to a bar and play that video game called "Match Game" in which you have to figure what is missing from a particular picture. For instance, there may be a picture of two houses side by side. One house is normal but the other house is missing certain things, like a chimney. It takes you a second, but you know something doesn't add up with the other house and eventually you figure out what is wrong with the picture. That's what alopecia universalis is like. When you see a guy with alopecia universalis, you know something is off but you can't quite put your finger on it. It's not the hair missing from his head, because a lot of guys shave their heads these days, and a guy with alopecia universalis just looks like one of them. No, it's the eyebrows. A person without eyebrows just doesn't look right. And therein is the rub to alopecia universalis. I suppose you could draw some eyebrows on your head, but that may cause more problems than it solves.

The grass is always greener. It is natural to be envious of other people, because it appears that their lives are better than ours for some reason or another. But when you dig a little deeper, you discover that everyone has problems to some degree. Now, if you were an Olympic swimmer, alopecia universalis might mean the difference between gold and silver; if you were a cancer patient, you would not have to endure the insult of losing your hair during the injury of radiation, because alopecia universalis would have already taken care of that. For a man with alopecia universalis, I would imagine he is thankful for the low maintenance and Olympic dreams his hairless head and body provide him, but upset with the fact that he has no eyebrows. While in a perfect world, I would have alopecia universalis exceptus eyebrowsis instead of male pattern baldness, I am not aware of such a medical condition. Thus, I just need to be comfortable in my own skin, and realize that a man with alopecia universalis has problems of his own.

Preemptive Action

During the earliest days of my journey, I told everyone who would listen that I am losing my hair. For one, I had already let the cat out of the bag on the day that will live in personal infamy when I blurted out to my classmates that autumn was setting upon my hair. But I had another reason: preemptive action.

Now, I know it is inappropriate to use military metaphors to refer to ordinary events. NFL players always talk about "going to war" on Sundays and my old boss used to "rally the troops" on slow Mondays by treating us all to mani-pedis at the local spa. And if you're a Democrat, I may be digging myself a deeper hole by borrowing a military term from the heart of the Bush Doctrine.

Nonetheless, in my case, preemptive action was a two-pronged strategy I implemented in my mid-twenties in order to make myself feel better about losing my hair. First, by telling people that I was losing my hair before it was obvious, I would lure people into boosting my confidence. People would invariably tell me that I was crazy for thinking that my hair was falling out. Whether friends, co-workers, family, belly dancers, or cab drivers, no one was safe from my pathetic and self-serving tactic.

If you ever meet me, or have already had the distinct pleasure of doing so, you will never confuse me with Richard Simmons. I do not exude energy and ebullience. One of my coaches in high school pulled me aside because my lack of enthusiasm on the court was troubling him and dispiriting team morale. And, when I interned for a stock brokerage firm in the summer of 1999, one of the brokers asked me to answer the phones with more "vim and vigor" and advised me that it was inappropriate to wear Chuck Taylor All-Stars in the office. After I looked up the meaning of "vim and vigor," I knew I didn't have what it took and walked away from that internship in my Chuck Taylor All-Stars.

However, when the mood struck, I surprised even myself with my ability to speak passionately about my fears and hopes regarding the hair on my head. Like a seasoned veteran of Community Theater auditioning for a role in a production of *Hamlet*, I became very dramatic and animated. As I recited the ever-captivating preamble of "there's something I have to tell you," I imagine those who listened to me thought I was breaking the news that I was diagnosed with testicular cancer or that I was coming out of the closet. My hands would flail about in the air in numerous and unpredictable directions as I explained the gut-wrenching feeling of losing a part of me to the gods of fate. Those with whom I shared my sob story would look at my large head, see a large amount of hair on my large head, and tell me that I had a screw loose because I was not balding. Nobody likes a drama queen, but like a cup of hot cocoa on a cold winter's day, it made me feel better.

The first prong of my strategy was equally effective on the fully-haired and the balding. However, when it came to taking preemptive action in the presence of the balding, I quickly learned that I had to be careful. Sure, I would choose dudes whose follicles were in worse shape than mine in order to make myself feel better. But in the process I would also unintentionally make the other guy feel worse about himself and risk alienation from those balding or bald persons with whom I compared myself.

The baldness community is kind of like *La Cosa Nostra*. Like I said before, I don't like to read, but now that *Breaking Bad* is over, quality television is at a minimum. So, recently, I figured "what the heck," and went to the library to check out *Underboss* by Sammy "the Bull" Gravano and Peter Maas. In the book, Sammy the Bull, a former high-ranking mobster, discusses the rules regarding introductions of made guys and non-made guys in the mafia:

Anyways, at the club, Toddo called Boozy over and said, 'Sammy is now a friend of ours.' It was the first time I was ever introduced like that. Chills just went up and down my spine. Lots of times, before I was made, I'd be with Toddo and maybe the way I was carrying myself, some old-timers who came down to see Toddo would say to him right in front of me, 'Sammy's a friend of ours?' and Toddo said, 'No, Sammy's a friend of mine.' Now I realized for the first time what Toddo was doing. It never meant anything to me up to that point.
[pp. 88-89.]

I know exactly how Sammy felt. I had a balding friend named Chris. I challenged him to a hair-off while I still had a ton of hair in the infant stages of my journey, and I felt like an outsider. He didn't know he was entering a contest, or that he was part of my preemptive action strategy. The contest was a simple yet enlightening affair. I would say "it really sucks that I'm losing my hair" and lift up the hair that covered my forehead and hid my receding hairline. My unwitting opponent replied, "Oh, really? Check this out," pointing to a hairline that was in full recession with only a thin layer of hair on top of his head. He was not pleased to have to be discussing his baldness, and he gave me a look of displeasure that I would even talk about my male pattern baldness when his hair loss was so much more pronounced than mine. If Chris and I were ever with a third party - another balding or bald man - I imagine Chris would have said, "This is Turney. He's a friend of mine." Not that I was eager to be introduced as a "friend of ours," or a member of the baldness community, but I soon brought an end to my hair contests. Just because I liked to openly talk about baldness doesn't mean other people do. Also, I didn't want to be shunned by the baldness community or whacked before I was officially recognized as a member.

The second prong of my preemptive action strategy was designed for the day when my head is full of bald spots for the whole world to see. People, at least those with whom I had implemented the first prong of my strategy, would not be shocked. They would not treat me any differently, I thought. They knew that I knew that I was losing my hair. I hoped that would quiet the whispers and the jokes. Now, I'm only showing signs of recession and increasing separation on the crown of my head, while there are men--and women--my age with much more severe hair loss than I have experienced. When I put my hair loss in perspective, I am doing pretty well considering I first started to lose my hair in 1999. But perhaps I am only fooling myself. I mean, I used to be able to tickle my balls with my bangs, and now, at best, my bangs can only tickle my forehead.

Perhaps my preemptive action was such a successful strategy that nobody dares comment on my hair loss. Based on past interactions with me, those in whom I confided my male pattern baldness may think that my ego and psyche are too feeble to handle the reality that my locks are no longer as thick and lustrous as they were when I was a younger man. I suppose that's what friends are for: to offer support and confidence. Friends are not as blatantly biased as mothers, who must always lie in order to make their children feel good about themselves, but it is sometimes difficult to know for sure whether a friend is being completely straight with you on sensitive topics.

I have aborted my preemptive action plan because even I was getting tired of listening to my self-pitying talk about hair loss, and because my hair is going to do what it is going to do. The plan served its purpose while in effect: I felt better about myself when people told me I wasn't going bald and when I compared myself to people with far fewer hairs on their heads than mine. I know that I am losing my hair. The hairs that have called it quits are not coming out of retirement, and those hairs will surely be followed by others just like them. The question is whether in the coming years the rate of attrition will be a sprinkle or a downpour.

The answer is, "Who cares?" Instead, just as I developed a coping mechanism in my early days of baldness when I implemented my preemptive action plan, I have come up with a revised strategy for the current and coming stages of my baldness: acceptance. You may be saying to yourself, "*Talk about beating a dead horse. How many times is this guy going to tell us about acceptance?!*", or "*Acceptance? How earth-shattering. What's he going to tell us next, that we shouldn't cry over spilt milk?*" Say what you will, but hey, when I spill milk I just calmly pour myself another glass. And, yes, acceptance is my solution to male pattern baldness.

That is how I will quiet the whispers and jokes about my baldness. I will no longer openly complain about losing my hair. Instead, I will be the first to crack a joke about my hair loss when the time is right. That will put the people around me at ease.

Lightheartedness about one's handicap is a great way to deter people from feeling sorry for you and to let people know that you accept your circumstances. I learned this from my friend Tom, who was paralyzed from the waist down after a pogo stick accident a few years ago and has been confined to a wheelchair ever since. He draws stares everywhere he goes, but he takes it all in stride. Every opportunity he gets, he will turn people's stares into laughter by telling a knee-slapper about always having a place for hookers to sit or about his antics in handicap stalls. I will carry that lesson with me on my journey. With it, I shall win people over by letting them know that, like dying only being hard on the living, going bald is only hard on those who are not balding. "It's pretty cool that Turney can joke about going bald. He kind of makes me want to go bald, too," my haired associates might say. Or maybe not. But by accepting my fate, I can show the outside world that I am not ashamed of my baldness. I can do my part in the fight for bald equality and the non-bald will come to accept the bald, balding and receding alike, as we are. Sometimes it helps to have a plan. Just ask that guy who got stuck between two rocks for 127 hours and decided to cut his arm off.

What a Bargain

During the early days of my journey I would also often engage in bargaining--the third stage of grief. I said to myself and others that my only hope was to keep my hair until I turned 30, or until I got married. At 24, 30 seems to be a distant age that, like marriage, marks the beginning of the end. I figured if life was going to be over anyway, it would not matter if I did not have hair.

In my younger days, I would look at bald and balding men and contemplate what it would be like with their heads of hair. I would stand in line at the bagel shop on Sunday mornings or ride the subway to and from work and judge other men's scalps for desirability. If it was all right for Jennifer Jason Leigh to copy Bridget Fonda's look in *Single White Female*, was I not entitled to stalk bald men on the subway?

"I couldn't go around looking like that," I might internally respond to a decidedly unflattering case of male pattern baldness. Or, "That wouldn't be so bad," might have been my attitude toward another, more appealing bald head. During my research, I might have also spotted a man in the crowd who I suspected had hair plugs or a toupee. "At least I'm not *that* guy," I would say as I kept my chin up. But such sightings would distract me from judging balding heads of hair I would actually like to have down the road, because when you see a man you suspect is wearing a really convincing toupee, you can't concentrate on anything else and you want to ask him if he's wearing a toupee to confirm your suspicions.

Unfortunately, social etiquette dictates that you leave such men's hair status to your imagination and good judgment. It's like encountering a really fat woman who looks pregnant. You may like to ask her how far along she is, or if she's having a boy or a girl, but you don't want to risk the uncomfortable moment that would ensue if it turns out that she is not actually pregnant. She may be pregnant, but if I can avoid a slap in the face from, or being sat on by, a 300-pound woman, I will. Despite my curiosity, I hold back from directly asking fat women if they are pregnant, and from inquiring whether pluggers or ruggers are masking their male pattern baldness. Besides, some of life's mysteries are more intriguing when left unsolved.

During my assessments of bald and balding men, I would only judge the hair of men like me: pale and of Anglo-Saxon descent. Black men could not provide a suitable mental image unless I suddenly decided that tanning salons were socially and personally acceptable and made appointments with regularity. Most of the time, I was curious to see how other pale faces carried the shaved head, or close-cropped style. Black men always look great with a shaved head, but that is not necessarily so for the white man. Head shape is crucial.

As it turns out, I found my bald idol, not on the subway, but on the silver screen. Since the best roles are generally reserved for fully haired superstars like Brad Pitt, Leonardo DiCaprio, or Gary Busey, I was a little shocked that I could find the ideal white bald man while eating pretzel bites at the theater. He is able to pull off the shaved-head-with-stubble look despite obvious signs of baldness because he has a head that is shaped so as to promote acceptability. His name is Jason Statham. He's not a household name in America, or anywhere else that I know of, and he wasn't the first bald or balding actor to get substantial roles, but he's been in some decent movies as a street tough or action star, including *Lock, Stock, and Two Smoking Barrels, Snatch,* and the *Transporter* movies. All right, the *Transporter* movies weren't that great, but here's to you, Jason Statham, for being a badass while being bald.

I also bargained with myself when I was in my early and mid-twenties by praying that I could just hold onto my hair until I found a wife. In my view, once I got married, my wife would have no choice but to stay with me. It is not an uxorial duty to remain married to a man who loses his hair after you tie the knot, but the last time I checked, baldness is not grounds for divorce.

As I said earlier, I was able to find "the one" after several failed relationships and frequent soul-searching. It was November 2009. The economy was in the tank and unemployment hovered around 10% in this country. I had a job, but it didn't pay well, I lived with my parents, and still had no concrete career plan after spending several tens of thousands of dollars on a law degree and watching law firms hand out pink slips by the thousands. So what better time to propose to your girlfriend, right?

Although my now-wife, Aisling, and I had been dating for about two years, I had never met her parents because they lived in Ireland. Aisling had no idea I was going to propose--probably assuming I was content with my mother doing my laundry for the rest of my life--so I had to discretely track down her parents' phone number from one of her sisters. I had planned to propose to her during our Thanksgiving dinner alone together, so I called her parents about a week in advance. It was a Saturday afternoon in America, Saturday evening in Ireland. My fingers were shaking as I pushed unfamiliar buttons on the phone, my stomach was in knots, and I hadn't really prepared any notes. Her father picked up the phone, and luckily knew who I was and had received some good reviews of me from Aisling. As a bonus, he was drunk, or at least sounded drunk, and gave his blessing without asking me the question I had been dreading: "How do you plan to support our daughter?" After dodging that bullet, he passed me to his wife, who called me "Bernie" several times and said how wonderful it was that I was going to marry their daughter.

Relieved, I was able to talk my way into a discount on a nice-sized rock in the back seat of a jeweler's car in Pennsylvania, and started to plan the details of my proposal. Plan A was to go to Wal-Mart to buy a diamond chip about the size of eye sleep, kneel down after dinner, and trick her into thinking she would have to wear a tiny diamond from Wal-Mart for the rest of her life, before presenting her with the real ring. Plan A fell through when her brother called her the day before Thanksgiving to say that he would be joining us for dinner. Despite what John Ritter and Suzanne Somers may have felt, to me, three's a crowd, so I needed a Plan B.

I had to improvise without much warning, so I wracked my brain for ideas both devious and romantic, and tried to remain calm. We were going to meet each other at Wegman's grocery store near Princeton after work on Wednesday to shop for food for Thanksgiving. She grew up in Rochester, NY, where Wegman's was

An Eagle Soars

founded, and would constantly rave about the quality of Wegman's, so I figured I would propose to her there. I mean, what girl wouldn't want to get engaged in a grocery store?

You can imagine how crowded a grocery store is the day before Thanksgiving, but I somehow had to pick a spot where I would not draw a crowd. While my past antics at fraternity parties and Bingo parlors would suggest otherwise, I do not like to make a scene. This wasn't my first Thanksgiving, so I knew that people would not be swarming the cereal aisle of the store. After all, it's turkey and stuffing, not turkey and Fruit Loops. Plus, I knew that there are surveillance cameras in the store so I thought I would later be able to get footage of the proposal.

But why would I, unlike the rest of America, need to go to the cereal aisle? Fiber One granola bars, that's why. I love the Oats and Chocolate Fiber One bars, and have been eating one every day after lunch for many years. Aisling knows how much I love Fiber One bars, and despite the benefits of fiber, Fiber One bars also cause what is known in the medical biz as intestinal gas. She knows this well also. They make me rip 'em all day long, and she has had to bear the brunt of these attacks all too often. "Hey, do you mind if we stop by the cereal aisle before we check out?," I asked. "Cereal aisle? What could you possibly need from the cereal aisle for Thanksgiving? Don't tell me. Fiber One bars? Oh, no!," she exclaimed.

So, Plan B was to take my act to the sparsely populated cereal aisle where Fiber One bars reside. But I told her that I was going to give her a break and make a switch to some other healthy dessert bar. Shocked that I was going to turn my back on the Fiber Ones I had craved for so long, she was able to collect herself and eagerly help me find an alternative with more socially and environmentally-friendly effects. If I know Aisling, I know she loves to talk, so I let her ramble on about candidates to replace Fiber One bars, and when she finally came up for air and turned around, I was on my knee with the ring held out in front of me. After shrieking "Oh, my god" several times, jumping up and down, and asking if the ring was real, she finally said yes, and I turned to the surveillance camera to give it a thumbs-up and a wink. I had taken the plunge, but the damned surveillance camera was broken that day so my showmanship went unrecorded. While I was disappointed the moment was not caught on tape, I was even more disappointed that

I had not been able to seize the opportunity to walk away with several free boxes of Fiber One bars.

As it happens, my life didn't end when I turned 30 or--believe it or not--even when I got married. I wasn't able to keep all of my hair when I reached those milestones, but somehow I survive. I could just give up, and let myself go. I could stop exercising, wear full-body sweats in public, and watch home movies of my former self with more hair, instead of going to antique auctions or showcasing my moves on the dance floor. But I choose not to. I will continue to wear business casual pants and shirts with collars, pump those 10-pound dumbbells, and dance like there is no tomorrow. My hair will continue to fall out, but I shall soar on my journey. I may have to watch more romantic comedies and eat less Fiber One bars than I'd like, but I will still muster the strength to soar on my journey. That is the best bargain I can make with myself.

Should I Fire My Hair Before It All Quits?

"I fired my hair before it quit." That's what Sam Madison, a former NFL cornerback, once told a reporter who asked him why he shaved his head. In other words, Sam was losing his hair naturally, so he got rid of the rest of it before male pattern baldness could. Like I said before, the shaved head look works for someone like Sam Madison because he is black and has a nicely shaped head; I am white and appear to have an oddly shaped head. Could *I* successfully sport the shaved head look if I so choose? I may have learned the answer to that question a few years back.

It was the summer of 1998, right after my freshman year of college. Tech stocks were taking the world by storm, Myanmar was known as Burma, Britney Spears was #1 on the charts, and Mark McGwire and Sammy Sosa were #1 in our hearts. The sky was the limit.

I lived with five other people in a house on Martha's Vineyard's Chappaquiddick Island. I held three part-time jobs simultaneously that summer. For one job, I bagged groceries and fetched shopping carts at *Super Fresh*. I once bagged groceries for the former NBA player Juwan Howard after he and his entourage racked up a $1000 bill. As I wondered how someone could possibly drop $1000 in one trip to the grocery store, I then started to wonder how someone could possibly drop $1020 in one trip to the grocery store, as Juwan kindly tipped me a $20 bill for bagging all of his goods. I mean, I've never tipped a bag boy. Have you?

I also worked as a short-order cook at the Chappaquiddick

Beach Club, where parts of the movie *Jaws* were filmed. I made a BLT that knocked people's socks and Speedos off.

But my favorite job that summer was a gig I had storing bales of hay on a farm on Chappaquiddick. My friend Farley and I would follow the baling machine in a truck and load up the bales to take to the barn for storage. Our supervisor was a free-spirited white guy with dreadlocks in his early 40s named Kevin, who actually made a country album entitled, "Hay Day." I still have a copy, but I don't think I've ever been in the mood to listen to it after Kevin fired me for driving the hay truck through a chicken coop.

Of course, it wasn't all work and no play for me that summer. No, I found time to unwind. I'm a simple man, with simple pursuits. So, my favorite pastimes that summer were Whiffle ball and Trivial Pursuit. I had some pretty intense Trivial Pursuit battles with my roommate Matt. Matt and I went to the same college, so if the suits at the admissions office got it right, one would imagine that we were intellectual equals. I wouldn't play with just any chump off the street--I needed a challenge. Matt was the perfect opponent because we shared a thirst for noetic stimulation *and* Jim Beam. And when you put the two together on the Trivial Pursuit board, there's no telling where the night would lead.

We followed the rules provided by the good folks who invented the game, but we added our own wrinkle. If you are familiar with the game, you know that the object is to correctly answer questions until you collect six wedges that correspond to the six categories and correctly answer an additional question once you reach the center of the board. The game itself was stimulating enough, but we decided to spice things up even more by rewarding a person with a shot of Jim Beam and a bong rip each time he earned a wedge. The other person would do the same in the spirit of friendly competition and to ensure that we remained at similar mental capacities. Well, on one lazy night in August, we decided to raise the stakes. We were neck and neck, with each of us having earned five wedges. One of us, I don't remember who, suggested that the loser would have to shave his head. It sounded like a great idea at the time--Jim Beam can make a lot of dumb things sound great--so we shook hands to consummate the deal. As we shook hands, I was already preparing my victory speech and picturing Matt with a bald head, and I'm sure he was doing the same.

High drama ensued, and you could see the beads of alcohol-filled sweat roll down our faces as we reached to the depths of our trivial knowledge banks for the right to keep our hair. We rolled the die and considered our questions with purpose. We were both in need of the pink wedge, which in the original Genus Edition of *Trivial Pursuit* was Arts and Entertainment. Now, this game was made in 1983, only a few years after Matt and I were born. I had watched my fair share of *Leave it to Beaver* reruns and had seen *Casablanca* once, but you don't learn about old movies and television in school or on the street like you do material covered by other categories like History, Science, and Geography. Thus, Matt and I acknowledged--and experience proved--that Arts and Entertainment was the weakest category for both of us, as it included pop culture questions more within the realm of knowledge of our parents' generation. And it took a while for one of us to earn a pink wedge, as we both answered numerous pink questions incorrectly. I mean, who under 60--or anyone for that matter--knows who played Tonto on the television show *The Lone Ranger*, or which movie won the second Oscar for Best Picture?![16]

As the night grew darker, we were both drained mentally from the grueling tests to which we subjected our brains, and physically from so much air guitar when Lynyrd Skynyrd's *Free Bird* came on the stereo at one point. We could have declared the game a draw, but we forced ourselves to finish the game.

I do not consider myself a sore loser, but the trivia gods were smiling upon Matt that evening as he got the luck of the draw and answered the easiest questions known to man to win the game, and I repeatedly got stumped by some of the hardest entertainment questions in the universe. I'm not a sore loser at all.

I honor my bets, and since Trivial Pursuit and dishonor don't mix, I replied, "Clippers" when Matt asked me whether I would prefer he used clippers or scissors to carry out my end of the bargain. The way I saw it, I wanted Matt nowhere near me with a pair of scissors at that point. It was tough enough losing at Trivial Pursuit; it would be even harder to accept my loss with one eye. But in a true show of friendship--or a true testament to the power of Jim Beam--Matt decided that he, too, would shave his head. He

---

[16] John Todd played Tonto and *The Broadway Melody* won the second Best Picture Oscar, in 1930.

An Eagle Soars

chose clippers as well.

When we awoke in the morning, we looked at each other and wondered what we had done. Last I remembered I had a full head of hair. Now it was all gone. Well, almost. Neither of us went to beauty school, and we wouldn't have put our previous night's work in our portfolios if we decided to apply. We each had random scraps of unshorn hair on our heads and looked like someone had attempted to shave our heads while drunk.

We cleaned each other up and then hit the streets of Martha's Vineyard. In 1998, in Martha's Vineyard, two white guys walking around with shaved heads seemed out of place. To on-lookers, we probably appeared to be neo-Nazis looking to start a rally, or at least that's what it felt like. The stares were piercing, there were no "how do you dos," and the service was not done with a smile. We tried to grab a bite to eat at a local restaurant. I had an itch only a bucket of fried chicken could scratch. However, as Matt and I stepped up to the counter to place our orders, we were told that, "We don't serve your kind here," and were asked to leave. "Our kind? What does that mean?," we wondered.

I had seen other white guys with shaved heads in the mid-to-late 1990s, but such a look was usually carried by someone who wanted to keep Hitler's dream alive or had contracted AIDS. The shaved head had yet to hit the mainstream, and Matt and I then knew what Miles Standish must have felt like when he landed on Plymouth Rock. We were not welcomed with open arms. Michael Jordan had begun to shave his head by then. But *he's* Michael Jordan and can do whatever he wants. Plus, no one would confuse him with a neo-Nazi.

I'd like to shake the hand of the first bald man who blazed the trail for the rest of us by helping to break up neo-Nazis' monopoly on the shaved head. But I would blaze my own trail by putting out my left hand for the shake. In America, it is custom to greet others with a right hand shake because most Americans are right-handed.[17] Therein lies the problem. I imagine most right-handers get through the day by using their right hands to pick their noses, wipe their butts, pet stray dogs, and masturbate. All the while, the left hand remains unmolested and untarnished. The odds are that

---

[17] An estimated 89% of Americans are right-handed.

you have shaken, and will shake hands, with many more right-handed people than left. That is why I submit that Americans should make the switch from greeting each other with our right hands to our left hands, and I will get the ball rolling when I finally track down the Meriwether Lewis of the male pattern baldness-induced head shave.

I didn't let the stares and snubs get me down that summer. I enjoyed the freedom and the low maintenance provided by my new hairstyle. I didn't like the possibility of being known around town as a neo-Nazi, but I didn't have to comb my hair in the morning and I could shower if I chose to, and no one would be the wiser if I chose not to. And even if people caught on, I would pretend to be European. I can do a pretty convincing French accent. As people would converse with me, they would say afterward, "Wow, that guy reeks. But it's customary in his country not to shower regularly. I wonder if he knows Gerard Depardieu?"

But on that first summer's day when I went out in public with my new 'do, I soon learned the importance of sunscreen on a bald head. I developed these huge welts on my head that would ooze with pus, and my scalp would peel for days to come. The sun became less of a tormentor as stubble accumulated on my head, but just like that time I cornered a skunk in my backyard and had to sit in a bathtub full of tomato juice for 5 hours, I learned a valuable lesson that day: A bald man, whether by nature or by choice, should never walk under the sun without protection.

Some people said I looked like a cancer patient, but one of my roommates' moms came for a visit and made me feel otherwise. She was obese. She was also a very religious woman--a born-again Christian I believe--so I think she *had* to be nice and friendly. She didn't try to make me see the light of God, but she did help me see the light of baldness. After we were introduced, we got to talking about my head. My head has been a regular topic of conversation throughout my life due to its size. Kids would knock me on the playground by calling me "big head," my sister liked to call me "basketball head," and I always had to bring my own helmet to Little League games because none of the ones supplied by the coach would fit. So it was not out of the ordinary for my head to take center stage, and I helped move it in that direction on that day with my shaved head.

I offered her one of my signature pina coladas, but she told me the only alcohol that ever touched her lips was the blood of heaven during Communion, and instead opted for apple juice. I decided then that I would leave Jim Beam out of the story of how my head became shaved, and told her that I was just trying out a new look. She told me that it "fit me" and that I had "such a nice head." She didn't know it, but in that five-minute conversation, she made me feel like a million bucks. I don't know if she was telling me the truth or not, because even though the Bible does not condone lying, she was a rather large woman who probably empathized with people with physical abnormalities, but she also gave me the confidence to shave my head when enough hair has fallen out naturally. So, like Sam Madison, I might just fire my hair before it all quits.

No Hair? Who Cares?

Hair serves no truly important purpose. It is not in the category of body parts or features that promote life or prevent death. If you get shot in the heart, you're dead. If you get shot in the hair, you're going to live. It's as simple as that.

If you spend a lot of time out in the sun, hair can prevent sunburn. If you live in Siberia, hair can protect you from the cold. I mean, look at Rasputin. His hair probably wasn't just there to promote the lunatic look he was going for. Yes, hair can be a nice bonus, but it's more of a luxury than a necessity. If you frequently comb the beaches of Florida with a metal detector and you are a bald man, you just have to remember to apply suntan lotion to your head. If you plan on going ice fishing in Canada and you also happen to be bald, put on a hat. There are many different styles from which to choose.

Admittedly, though, a full head of hair can be easy on the eyes. In law school, I wrote a paper on historic preservation in the United States. Of course, I got an A+--but enough about me. As a country, we value an individuals' property rights, but we also get a sense of civic pride from buildings that played an important role, or housed a pivotal figure, in our country's development. In comes historic preservation.

Under the Fifth Amendment to the United States Constitution, the government has a right to take a person's property for a public purpose as long as the government provides just compensation. Well, the law of eminent domain so favors the government that the government is not actually considered to have taken property in most instances unless it deprives the property owner of all economically viable use of his land. The government may exercise its police power in restricting a property owner's use of his land by acting in the interest of the public's health, safety, or welfare. In terms of historic preservation, the government's police power is so broad now as a result of legislation and court decisions that it may restrict the use of a particular property or a group of properties solely on the basis of aesthetics. Thus, if the government believes your property is of historic or architectural significance, it can tell you that it won't let you repaint your house the pink color you've always dreamed of because such a change would detract from the aesthetics of the neighborhood or devalue the importance of your house. Beauty is in the eye of the beholder, so the aesthetics justification provides the government with significant leeway. Having grown up in a historic district in Princeton, New Jersey, which includes the house in which Albert Einstein lived, I can appreciate the aesthetic benefits of historic preservation. While having your property designated as an historic site or as part of an historic district can be burdensome, it is nice to know that, due to the historic preservation movement, certain historically significant homes or buildings will not fall into disrepair or fall into the hands of commercial developers who will tear them down and erect IKEAs.

Sometimes I wish the government were more involved in the historic preservation of people's hair. Just as the government would not allow the Washington Monument or Edgar Allen Poe's home to decay due to neglect or indifference, maybe it should not allow people's hair to decay due to genetic predispositions. Forget finding a cure for the common cold. No, the government should devote more resources to finding a cure for male pattern baldness.

When I look in the mirror, I see a wealth of history. My hair and I were at Camden Yards for Cal Ripken's 2632nd and final game of his Iron Man streak for the Baltimore Orioles; my hair and I introduced rollerblades to Beach Haven, New Jersey in 1988; and my hair and I were among the first billion people served by

McDonald's. Does that not count for something? Why is the government not making an effort to designate my hair as an historic site? Perhaps if I start a petition in my neighborhood and get enough people to state that they would like me to keep my hair, the government will see what it can do to preserve my hair. Then again, they may then place restrictions on my hair such that I could not get highlights or frosted tips. Yet as hard as it would be to resist the temptation to get highlights or frosted tips, I think that would be a fair trade and that I could live within such parameters.

Since there is no scientific cure for baldness, and since the government couldn't care less whether my hair falls out or not, it is not now possible to preserve my hair despite the rich history it has witnessed and contributed to. I can accept that. I may get nostalgic and sentimentally reflect on the fuller days my hair and I had together, like a hippie does a two-day LSD trip at Woodstock, but I have come to terms with my hair follicles' fate. I was not meant to be among the 50% of men who keep all of their hair until at least the age of 50. I suppose I could try to preserve what is now on top of my head by getting castrated. I'd rather not, though.

Who am I to complain about losing my hair? I heard a story about a woman, Charla Nash, who was attacked--mauled, actually--by her friend's pet chimpanzee in Connecticut in 2009. In its youth, the chimp starred in Old Navy and Coca-Cola commercials. The chimp was probably adorable when it was young. Unfortunately, Father Time waits for no one, and like that kid who played Nicholas on *Eight is Enough*, the chimp grew up and wasn't cute anymore. And like most former child stars, the chimp was probably angry that the job offers weren't coming its way anymore. Well, Charla was in the wrong place at the wrong time--supposedly her friend asked her to come over to try to help calm the chimp down during a fit of rage--and suffered devastating injuries when the chimp assailed her. Some friend. As a result of the attack, she lost her eyes, nose, lips, and both of her hands except for one thumb. She wore a veil to spare others from the horrible damage she suffered until she got a face transplant. And I worry about losing some hair?!

As a tall man on a journey that may end in complete baldness, I took some comfort in a *USA Today* article I read. The article concluded that CEOs would rather be bald than short:

> CEOs say being bald doesn't impede success and, given a choice, it's better to be bald than short. So widely held is this conventional wisdom among top executives that when asked to choose, most CEOs say they'd take 2 more inches of height over a full head of Robert Redford hair.

> 95% of the 74 [CEOs] who responded said, if given a choice, they would rather be bald than short. More telling is that the 31 CEOs who identified themselves as bald or 'headed in that direction' in the unscientific survey were unanimous in saying that being vertically challenged is more detrimental to an aspiring executive's career.

> [March 14, 2008, Del Jones.]

It's nice to know that I could just become a CEO if all my hair falls out. I don't have any business experience, but I'm tall. Where do I sign up? I also just need to take solace in the fact that a full head of hair, while aesthetically pleasing, does not serve any truly important purpose. Besides, I can think of a lot of things that are worse than being bald. Like getting mauled by a chimpanzee.

A Real Head-Scratcher

My head itches. A lot. I have dandruff, which I prefer to call "dry scalp," but the shampoos I have bought to combat this problem have been largely ineffective. Thus, I am left to my own devices, otherwise known as my fingers.

It is human nature to scratch an itch. Of course, there are certain regions of the anatomy that Emily Post would advise against scratching in public. However, scratching is delightful because it relieves suffering and provides a welcome, if cheap, thrill. As a result, I find myself scratching my head on a regular basis. Sometimes I scratch my head when I wonder how I could live in a country in which *NCIS* is the top-rated show on television, or as I ponder whether the parents of former major league pitcher Dick Pole realized just how cruel *and* redundant they were being when they named him, or as I reflect on how I could have possibly thought it was all right for me to wear a mesh tank top so often in the summer of '95, but it's usually because my "dry scalp" is acting up again, and I could use a cheap thrill whenever one is available.

However, the latter form of head scratching is a double-edged sword. For while scratching my head provides relief and pleasure, the forecast also calls for a snowstorm with a chance of intermittent hair fall. Sure, that hair would fall out eventually even if I did not scratch my head, but the head scratching accelerates the hair's separation from my scalp and creates an immediate distraction.

I wouldn't call myself a "go-getter" or a "work machine," and none of my nicknames over the years has included either of these monikers. Don't get me wrong--I still know how to put in an honest day's work. But on one recent workday, there was a report that just had to wait to get done, because I had an itch on my head that needed to be scratched. I willingly obliged, but to my dismay, a couple of my hairs decided to leave the nest. As I brushed the snow and strands of hair from my desk, I was struck with a feeling of nostalgia and a reminder of my fate.

I harkened back to a time when my hair was as full of life as Katie Couric in the morning. I cracked a smile, put my hands behind my head, and leaned back in my ergonomically-correct chair as I remembered some of the good times my hair and I used to have. There were all those car rides we took together with the windows down, letting the wind unleash it's fury on us as we went wherever the road took us. Like lovers in the park on a summer's day, I didn't care who saw us in those days because I knew there was nothing to hide. My hair loved me and I loved it right back. There was a time when there was no risk of exposing a receding hairline, because there wasn't one; there were no thinning hairs, because the miniaturization process had not yet begun. And when the windows finally went up, my hair would fall back into place without any help from me. My hair was like a dog that went to obedience school and passed with flying colors.

Sure, my hair and I had some good times. But the halcyon days are coming to an end. Nowadays I am not so quick to press the down button in order to open a car window. However, I have learned a trick for when the temperature is right, because I still enjoy the fresh air as much as the next guy. I brush my hair from right to left, as I believe any right-handed man should. Thus, when I am driving, I find that if I open the passenger's side window halfway or less, I am able to enjoy some fresh air and the sounds of the street without detrimental consequences for my hair. Under such circumstances, I am able to control the extent of the wind's reach and force so that it gently hits my hair without causing too many hairs to fall out of place.

As much as I would like to fully open both the driver's side and passenger side windows, the risk is too great. For under such a scenario, the wind would attack me from both sides in such a way as to drive my hair to the center of my forehead to form an unsightly and un-businesslike v-shape with a lot of bare scalp visible along my temples. In addition to such feelings of nakedness, I would have to do some maintenance work after the windows went back up because my hair no longer returns to its original place on command. And since I don't carry a comb with me--unless you're the Fonz or have an afro, who does?--I play it safe and settle for rolling down just the passenger's side window.

By the time I came to, several minutes had passed and I knew that that report wasn't going to write itself. As I unclasped my hands and returned my seat to the upright position, I was glad for the break but also perturbed that I had lost my train of thought as I reflected on my hair days of yore. While I was able to collect myself, the idea that I can be so easily distracted is unsettling. However, I am confident that with time, self-control, and a cure for my dandruff, er, "dry scalp," my head scratching will be merely a relief and a thrill, and I will be able to enjoy a good head scratch without letting it distract me from the task at hand. Besides, as Ray Lewis said after he retired from football, only a fool trips on what's behind him.

The Journey Continues

To me, there are three stages of male pattern baldness, and they're kind of like Dante's Divine Comedy. There is the receding stage, which is like Paradiso; there is the balding stage, which is like Purgatorio; and, there is the bald stage, which is like Inferno. Thus, a journey to baldness may include several stops.

In the receding stage, hair loss is confined to the front of the head. The hairline moves uniformly back, very gradually. Thus, in this stage, you will never suffer any dramatic or heavy hair loss in a short amount of time. You may never truly experience the full effects of the male pattern baldness phenomenon. Indeed, the fully haired may even consider you to be one of their own. That is Paradiso.

The next stage--balding--is the Purgatorio of male pattern baldness. However, while in Dante's scheme of things Purgatorio was the place where people waited to find out if they would be going to heaven or hell, the balding man no longer has a chance to live happily ever after in the Paradiso of male pattern baldness (receding). The balding man has reached the point of no return to Paradiso. He can either stay in Purgatorio, or move on to the bald stage, Inferno. Those are the balding man's only options.

What separates the balding man from the receding man is the separation between his hairs. As explained above, the receding man's hair moves up the scalp in a uniform and gradual manner. Each hair tows the line, and no hair is left behind. For the balding man, his hair loss is less predictable. The balding stage gives male "pattern" baldness a bad name, because it seems as if there is no predictable pattern when it comes to the balding stage. Balding heads are kind of like snowflakes – no two are exactly the same. The scalp becomes the picture of chaos, as the balding man does not know what his hair will do. All he knows is that his hairs are moving further and further apart from each other, and his hair is becoming thinner. That is something with which the receding man does not have to contend. The receding man experiences no pronounced separation and the hair that remains is generally thick.

The bald man has reached the end of his journey. He has arrived. It may have taken many years, but he need not worry about more hair falling out and may hopefully enjoy some peace and quiet. He's earned it. The bald man is in the Inferno of male pattern baldness. But hold on. Although the bald man has nothing left to lose, he has so much to gain. He can now move on with his life. He does not have to sit around and twiddle his thumbs while he waits for his hair to fall out; he does not have to worry that Thanksgiving dinner will be ruined because his hair fell into the stuffing; and he will no longer have to buy *Draino* every time he goes to the grocery store. Those days are over. Like the New York City Marathon runner who finishes the race despite getting colossal cramps and shitting himself, the bald man deserves to be saluted. You see? Hell doesn't have to be so bad.

My hair in general does not yet look thin, but there is a good amount of separation between my hairs. I do not fit neatly into my own categories because I look like a receding man but feel like a balding man. My hair still appears to be in the receding stage because what remains is mostly thick and picks up the slack for the hair that has thinned or abandoned me. Upon close inspection, though, you can see that there is no uniformity in my hair loss. I have the outline of a Widow's Peak, but there is separation at the peak and there are remnants of hair along the sides of the peak. Thus, I do not consider myself a receding man. Instead, you will see that across my scalp there is a lot of elbowroom between my hair, and the hair on the crown of my head is starting to part like the Red Sea. I think it is this separation that separates me from a receding man and forces me to join the ranks of the balding in Purgatorio. Will I ever transition from balding to bald? I do not yet know the answer to that question.

Nonetheless, my journey continues. How do I know? It's hard

to miss. Everywhere I look, I see hair that has fallen from my head. When I wake up in the morning the first thing to greet me after "*Boomer and Carton*" on my alarm clock radio is a scattering of hair on my pillow. When I apply shampoo to my head, several hairs are consistently entangled around my fingers after having been genetically dislodged from my scalp. When I get out of the shower and dry off my head, what is that I see on my towel but another group of formerly live hairs? Thus, I am reminded of my journey on several occasions within the first fifteen minutes of each day.

Yes, the average person loses over 100 hairs a day, but since that's an average, some people lose more than 100 hairs a day, and for those who have not inherited male pattern baldness or some other hair loss condition, most, if not all of those lost hairs will grow back. I do not count how many hairs fall out of my head each day. My boss would probably frown upon it. All I know is that hair falls from my head consistently throughout the day and night and that there's not much I can do about it.

As my hair fell out over the years, I developed techniques to create the illusion of a more expansive head of hair than I actually had at the time I employed a particular technique. Like an artist (more like a con artist), I would spend many minutes in the morning sculpting my hair in front of the mirror. The most common sculpting technique in my bag of tricks was something I liked to call "the cascade effect."

In a waterfall, water travels downstream, reaches a cliff, and majestically flows to another body of water below, and the resulting cascade effect is not only one of nature's finest musical instruments, but one of its most picturesque phenomena as well. The waterfall is so wondrous that it provides the perfect screen saver for daydreams at work, idyllic inspiration for those interested in adopting the ancient Chinese art of feng shui in their homes or gardens, and its image offers timely inducement for those uncomfortable situations in which you get stage fright at a public urinal.

I never thought I could spend so much time in front of a mirror. But sometimes I surprise myself, like when I'm able to pass by a group of Christmas carolers and resist the urge to join them in song.

And what a surprise those waterfall days were. Like a Guido preparing for a night of fist pumping and sexual harassment at a Jersey Shore club, I spent an unconscionable amount of time staring into a mirror in the morning for many years. Time that could have been spent learning Swahili or doing a few reps on the Ab Roller before work was instead misdirected toward efforts to create the appearance of a full head of hair.

In came the cascade effect. After I got out of the shower, I would dry my hair thoroughly with a towel. If I got carried away with the hair drying, I would sometimes pull a muscle in my neck, the effects of which would last for days and leave me unable to turn my head from side to side. Thus, I had to find the right speed and angle at which to dry my hair in order to get the job done quickly but without putting at risk my ability to play *Pong* or line dance. If I avoided a neck strain, I might have winked at myself just to say "hello" or "nice job." If my hair was sufficiently dry, I would comb it with a brush from right to left, creating a part on the right side of my head. This would expose my hair loss for what it was--a great recession up the right side but with coverage on the left over to where the hair had been combed. I know what you might be thinking, but it was a regular comb job, not a comb-over. However, I would not be content with leaving my hair as such because, as I got deeper into my twenties, my hairline after such a comb job would look like a wheelchair ramp and the world would be able to see the stark separation that had developed between my hairs.

The cascade effect saved me from such despair. After reading that the average scalp has about two hundred hairs per square centimeter--and after looking up how to convert centimeters to a measurement I understand—I realized that only half this amount is needed to provide a semblance of coverage. I decided to put this factoid to the test and use it to my advantage. In order to create the appearance of a fuller hairline--or smaller forehead--I would use my fingers to finesse the hair on top of the right side of my head downward. So if the top of my head were a stream and my forehead a cliff, the hair that I coaxed from its resting place after combing would act as the waterfall and thus produce a cascade effect. But it was not easy to create the perfect cascade effect. I had to find a balance between forehead coverage and businesslike neatness. I could not sacrifice one for the other. And this took time.

Despite the inordinate amount of time I spent sculpting my hair in the mornings, the cascade effect always remained prone to the whims of Mother Nature. Thus, even if I spent 15 minutes perfecting the cascade effect, I could protect my hard and unnecessary work only as long as I stayed sheltered. As soon as I stepped outside, all bets were off. I'm talking about you, wind. While it's hard to show disdain for a cool breeze on a hot summer's day, I would have gladly sweated a little more if it meant that the wind would not have attacked my hair and disrupted my morning creation.

The wind always seemed to blow when I could least afford it. I remember a job interview I had in Washington, D.C. in 2008. I had done my homework on the company --and my hair. Before the interview, I stood before the mirror in my hotel room in order to create the cascade effect that would allow me to look sharp to be sharp. "Look sharp to be sharp" has been my motto since 1997, and all indications were that it was going to prove true once again during my interview. I had a pressed suit, shined shoes, the eye of the tiger, my lucky tie, and a hairstyle to mask the reality of my male pattern baldness. However, I forget one minor detail--that my nemesis, the wind, lurked in the streets of the District of Crime--and it unleashed its unforgiving fury on me as I walked the five blocks to the interview.

"Egad!," I gasped as my hair swooshed in every direction and turned the cascade effect into a natural disaster. "What am I to do?" I tried to remain calm, and as I climbed the stairs to my destination, I wondered if that was the first time I had ever used the word "Egad." I decided that I would ask the receptionist if I could use the bathroom--I would then be able to try to accomplish with my fingers and poor lighting the magic act I had pulled no more than a half hour before. However, as soon as I checked in with the receptionist, she informed me that my interviewers were waiting for me in the conference room. I had no choice but to enter my interview "as is" and hope no one thought that I just rolled out of bed.

I like to think that I didn't get the job because I didn't look sharp, and thus couldn't be sharp. The wind really threw me off my game that day, and it's like the wind left my brain as disheveled as the hair on my head. Without the calming influence of the cascade effect, I could not concentrate on the questions that were being asked, and I let the wind get the better of me. Hopefully, globing warming will put the wind in its place because I found out that throwing punches at the wind doesn't hurt it and only makes me look crazy.

After the interview, I vowed to part ways with the cascade effect. The wind is like an older brother who knocks down in one moment the house of cards or domino train you spent days putting together. Unless I could walk around with a contraption like The Boy in the Plastic Bubble used (but without the immune system issues), the wind would always have the upper hand. Unlike basketball coaches and Wall Street types, I will not resort to metrosexual products such as gel and hairspray. It is au naturel or bust. So when I wake up in the morning these days, I let nature take its course--no sculpting, no cascade effects--just me and a businesslike part that offers a daily progress report on my journey to baldness.

The Psychology of Hair Loss

Some people probably think I was crazy to care about losing my hair and for using *Propecia*. But given the popular views of baldness in this country, perhaps I was just crazy like a fox. I thought that losing my hair would make me look like less of a man, weak, and somehow a failure at life. And psychologists who have studied the psychological effects of male pattern baldness have discovered that many men share similar feelings as I had, and that those negative feelings of self-image and self-worth emanate both from our own perceptions and the perceptions of others.

In the literature I read on the psychological aspects and effects of male pattern baldness, I was thunderstruck by the work on the subject by Dr. Thomas F. Cash, a retired professor in the Department of Psychology at Old Dominion University. As I read Cash's studies, I no longer felt alone, and his work supported, if not validated, my seemingly paranoid behavior prior to my acceptance of baldness. Cash has produced several research papers on his findings regarding men's experiences with and attitudes toward hair loss, as well as the way in which the non-balding view people with male pattern baldness.

According to Cash, "[f]or many people, hair is a physical attribute that expresses individuality and is central to feelings of attractiveness or unattractiveness" and "hair loss can threaten one's sense of personal and social acceptability."[18] Cash supported these

---

[18] Cash T.F., The Psychology of Hair Loss and Its Implications for Patient Care. Clinics in Dermatology 2001;19:161-166.

conclusions with a non-clinical survey of 145 American men between the ages of 18 and 70 who did and did not have androgenetic alopecia.[19] Cash asked those men with male pattern baldness how that condition affected their daily lives, and this is what Cash discovered:

> Two thirds of the men wished for more hair. Sixty percent reported greater social self-consciousness. Sixty-two percent said that peers teased them about their hair loss. Forty-seven percent felt that they looked older than their age and worried about other people noticing their baldness. Forty-one percent said that their hair loss made them feel less attractive. Forty-six percent experienced frustration and helplessness about their hair loss. Comparisons of men with modest-to-moderate versus moderate-to-extensive [androgenetic alopecia] revealed that greater hair loss was associated with significantly higher levels of stress and distress about the condition. Men with more versus less extensive hair loss (59% vs. 31%) reported greater social and emotional adversities, revealed more mental preoccupation with their hair loss (69% vs. 54%), and made stronger efforts to cope with it (69% vs. 48%).[20]

Male pattern baldness psychologically affects some men more

---

[19] Cash, T.F., The psychological effects of androgenetic alopecia in men. J Am Acad Dematol 1992;26:926-931.

[20] Cash T.F., The Psychology of Hair Loss and Its Implications for Patient Care. Clinics in Dermatology 2001;19:161-166.

than others, and I will admit that for several years, I was self-conscious about my hair loss and exhibited many of the characteristics of what Cash calls a "vulnerability model."[21] According to Cash, there are certain factors that contribute to a man's susceptibility for negative feelings about his hair loss.[22] These factors include losing one's hair at a relatively early age, because a young man's "appearance is beginning to differ from [his] peers in an atypical and socially undesirable respect;" being single, because unattached men "feel that their attractiveness is diminishing and worsening their chances for dating and mating;" putting great stock into one's physical appearance; and seeking treatment to combat male pattern baldness, because men who seek treatment are more preoccupied with their hair loss than those who do not seek treatment.[23]

It's almost as if Cash had been talking about *me*. I started to slowly lose my hair at 21, I wasn't in a serious relationship for most of my twenties, I spent a good amount of time checking myself out in the mirror and consulting *GQ*, and I paid a visit to the doctor's office to discuss with him options to stop my hair loss. Thus, according to Cash, I was extremely vulnerable to negative feelings about my hair loss, and that vulnerability turned to reality for several years.

Perhaps not surprisingly, balding men have developed common coping mechanisms to deal with the stress caused by their hair loss.[24] Again, I must've had a nametag on or something, because it was like Cash was calling out to me as I read about typical coping strategies. The first coping method is compensation: a man with male pattern baldness may try to improve other physical characteristics--like pumping iron at the gym to build bigger arm muscles or by using a dick pump at home to build a bigger penis muscle--in order to counteract the fact that he is losing his hair.[25] For me, it was all

---

[21] Ibid.

[22] Ibid.

[23] Ibid.

[24] Ibid.

[25] Ibid.

about having the best looking quads in town. I once disappeared for a whole winter, holed up in my apartment with nothing but a Thighmaster and a dream. If you remember that Spandex shortage in the spring a few years ago, now you know why.

The second method is concealment. The greatest example of this method is the infamous comb-over to try to cover up one's baldness; another example is avoiding certain situations that may enhance the appearance of baldness, such as going out in public on a windy day or getting one's hair wet by doing cannonballs off the diving board.[26] For me, it was the "cascade effect."

The third method is compulsive behavior to make oneself feel better about one's appearance, like spending a lot of time fixing one's hair in front of the mirror or seeking reassurance from others about one's appearance.[27] For me, it was the "cascade effect" and the "preemptive action" strategy.

However, these common coping mechanisms may only provide temporary relief because they do not solve the underlying reality of hair loss and may only lead to bigger problems. It's like the guy who gets tennis elbow and goes to the doctor for help. Let's call this guy "Johnny," because all of the cautionary tales I've ever heard involve some guy named Johnny. The doctor gives Johnny a prescription for the opiate painkiller, Percocet. Well, Johnny learns that the Percocet only masks, but does not cure, the pain of his tennis elbow. Johnny scoffs at the notion of physical therapy, and instead pops Percocet with alacrity because he likes the way it makes his body feel. His tennis elbow isn't going anywhere, and he's been taking so much Percocet that he builds up a tolerance and eventually it just doesn't make him feel the way it used to. And before he knows it, Johnny starts chasing the dragon. And what does that make Johnny? A heroin addict with tennis elbow. See what a slippery slope coping mechanisms can be?

While Cash has studied the negative psychological consequences that may affect men who suffer from hair loss and the coping strategies they may adopt, Cash has also analyzed the effects of baldness on social impressions. And according to Cash's

---

[26] Ibid.

[27] Ibid.

research, many men, including me, rightfully believe that our baldness may adversely impact others' initial perceptions of us, and may compound the negative psychological consequences experienced by men with male pattern baldness.

In one study, Dr. Cash presented 18 pairs of photographs of balding and nonbalding men, who were matched based on age, race, and other physical characteristics, to 54 men and 54 women, who ranged in age from 18 to 66 years old.[28] The purpose of the study was to gauge the influence of male pattern baldness on the initial social perceptions of men by both sexes.[29] The results of the study would generally not be considered good news for men with male pattern baldness.

As noted by Cash,

[g]iven their equivalence on a variety of appearance factors other than the presence or absence of [male pattern baldness] the perceived differences between balding and nonbalding men confirm a generally deleterious social stereotype of balding. Hair loss produced social judgments of lower aesthetic appeal and fostered less favorable initial assumptions about what the men were really like personally. The personalities of balding men were thought to be weaker or less confident, less socially interesting, and less friendly. Their lives were assumed to be less happy and successful. Nor did balding men elicit feelings of personal likeability by others as readily as did nonbalding men. Perceptions of intellectual

---

[28] Cash, T.F., Losing Hair, Losing Points? Journal of Applied Social Psychology, 1990, 20, 2, 154-167.

[29] Ibid.

> capacity were not affected here by the presence or absence of hair loss. Finally, a full head of hair caused underestimating of actual age, while balding fostered estimates older than were accurate."[30]

As for the people whose opinions about their physical appearance men most generally care about--women--the results were mixed. When Cash analyzed the perceptions of women by dividing them into two age groups--a "young" group of women, ages 18-22, and an "older" group of women, ages 23-66--Cash found that "[f]emales in both age groups regarded the older balding men [35 years old or older] as less successful and physically less attractive than the nonbalding controls. The younger females also regarded younger balding men [35 years old or younger] as less intelligent, successful, likeable, and physically attractive than they regarded the nonbalding young men. In contrast, the older females perceived younger balding men as somewhat more intelligent, successful, and likeable, but not differentially physically attractive than nonbalding men."[31] So, if there is a silver lining to be found by younger men with male pattern baldness it is this: you may not have a great chance with cheerleaders, but you still have a solid chance with cougars. And there's nothing wrong with that.

Thus, Cash's study confirmed his hypothesis that "the presence or absence of male pattern hair loss exerts reliable effects on the initial social impressions of men by both male and female strangers."[32] And, unfortunately, this could be important, because as Cash notes, "appearance-cued first impressions may act as a funnel, through which other perceptions, expectations, feelings, and social behaviors are channeled."[33] Thus, just as Asian people must unfairly overcome such stereotypes as being bad drivers and not respecting the personal space of others, men with male pattern

---

[30] Ibid.

[31] Ibid.

[32] Ibid.

[33] Ibid.

baldness must rise above stereotypes such as being less likeable, less successful, less happy, and less confident than haired men.

Of course, a lot of stereotypes are true, and some balding men are indeed less likeable, successful, happy, and confident than their nonbalding counterparts. But this does not mean that men with male pattern baldness should just give up. On the contrary, if you are losing your hair, you need to get out there and do your damnedest to reverse the stereotypes that plague our kind. Sure, you should only surround yourself with people that accept you for who you are, but you will have interactions with people that don't have to accept you for who you are, and may, either consciously or subconsciously, judge you for the amount of hair on your head. As the Old Spice deodorant commercials used to claim, "you never get a second chance to make a first impression." And since, in my experience, deodorant companies have never failed to dole out reliable words of wisdom, men with male pattern baldness might just have to work a little harder to make the most of first impressions.

I was not crazy to think that the state of my hair has an impact on my interactions with other people. But I cannot allow such trifling matters to keep me from enjoying life. No, I'm still going to gleefully run around my house with just a t-shirt on like, Porky Pig; I'm still going to start my day off right with a half-hour poop in the morning; and I'm still going to laugh whenever I hear the word "poop," because, *goddamn*, it's funny.

Men can and will deal with their baldness however they so choose. I decided to finally accept my hair loss so I could stop wasting so much time worrying about it and so much money trying to stop or reverse it. So, bald men, I implore you to join me in the acceptance pool. The water's fine. Take it from me, because acceptance has had a wondrous effect on my life. I can now skip to the beat of confidence and know that no matter how much hair I may lose, I can still climb the highest mountain, sail the widest sea, and rollerblade the longest road.

I Have a Dream

My mother always said I could be whatever I wanted to be when I grew up. Well, my mother lied.

When I was 5, I wanted to be a professional break-dancer, or "B-Boy." Inspired by Michael Jackson's wardrobe and the break dancing craze that was sweeping the nation in 1983, my mom bought me a pair of black leather pants and a bandana and I went to work on making my dream a reality. However, on the first day, as I was practicing a move known as the "Skyscraper," my pants split in the back, I cried, and the B-Boy dream came to an end.

When I was 12, I wanted to be a professional baseball player. During one Little League game I stood at the plate to face Timmy Rogers, who was 6'2" and had a moustache like Tom Selleck. He hurled an 80-mile an hour fastball at my face, and that effectively ended my dreams of making the big leagues. Tennis, anyone?

When I was 17, I wanted to be an underwear model. I figured if Mark "Marky Mark" Wahlberg could parlay a troubled childhood into a gig with Calvin Klein, leading to a successful--if laughable--stint as a white rapper and a notable movie career, so could I. I had the troubled childhood part down, or at least I *caused* a lot of trouble as a child. However, when I went to a modeling agency in New York City for an audition, my hopes of seeing my scantily clad self on buses and subway station walls were quickly dashed. Apparently, I didn't have "the look," as I had failed to ever lift a weight or do a sit-up in my life, my head was too big, and my penis too small. I thought I could corner the boxers market, but with metrosexualism on the rise, there was a spike in demand for briefs, or "tighty-whiteys," and they needed someone who could fill them out. "But isn't that what socks are for?," I thought to myself. As I was shown the exit door, I looked on the bright side: *I haven't worn tighty-whiteys since I was four. They weren't all right then, and they're not all right now. That agency just did me a big favor.* Thus, the underwear model / white rapper / movie star dream came to an end.

When the first signs of male pattern baldness interrupted my worry-free life, I wanted to be a fully haired man for the remainder of my time on this earth. My hair and I had been through so much together: Who was there when I greeted the world as I exited my mother's stomach? (The doctors got one look at the size of my head and knew there was no way I was coming out naturally); who was there when I learned to read at age 2? (unfortunately, that fire didn't stay in my belly for very long as I've read about 10 books since then); who was there when I got detention all those times? (I believe I set a private school record for most detentions by age 9); who was there when I took it to funky town by ripping it up at the roller rink during Jenny Miller's 11th birthday party and held hands with the birthday girl? (After she saw my moves on the four-wheelers, I gotta say that I was a little shocked that the hand-holding wasn't accompanied by a kiss on the cheek); and, who was there when I unsuccessfully mounted a one-man grassroots campaign my freshman year of college to make turtlenecks socially acceptable for men? (Sometimes comfort must take precedence over pride). All of my hair, that's who! And I use the word "who" to refer to my hair because I regard my hair as a sentient being. Thus, when I talk about losing my hair, I am talking about losing a friend or a relative. If you have ever lost a friend or relative, you understand how difficult it can be.

My hair and I have been through thick together; now, we shall go through thin together. Who will be there when I'm an old, senile man? (son, just remember that I wiped your butt, so it's only fair that you wipe mine); who will be there when the New York Mets finally win another World Series in 2036? (if the Mets have not won another World Series by then, I shall say goodbye to my family and become a monk); and who will be there when I'm put six feet under? (if I run away and become a monk, not my family, that's for sure). Some of my hair, that's who!

To those hairs who stay, I salute you. For those who have left me and will leave me in the days to come, I do not hold any grudges. However, my dream of being a fully haired man for the rest of my life came to an end a long time ago. The show must go on, and I will not allow the major and minor events that I will experience in the future to be any different from the way they would have been if I had kept a full head of hair. Like the sentiment to which I alluded above, though, my forthcoming experiences sans all of my hair will be akin to the feelings one has when a lost loved one is no longer around to share in all that life has to offer.

One of my grandfathers died before my 16th birthday. He actually died before I was born. But legend had it that he was a very talented man. He had a day job, but moonlighted as an entertainer of sorts. He was known as "Babbles the Clown." Weddings, bar mitzvahs--any special occasion you could think of, he was the man for the job. He didn't do any tricks, like make balloon animals or juggle while riding around on a unicycle. But he had the gift of gab, and could bend any ear. If only he could have performed at my Sweet Sixteen party, I wonder if my life would have turned out differently. If the kids in town had known that Babbles was *my* grandfather, maybe they would have thought I was cooler. I don't know. It's kind of nice to think about.

Sure, I wish my grandfather could have been around to see me grow up, just like I would've preferred to have a full head of hair for the rest of my travels in life. But hey, I've got bigger fish to fry than worrying about the amount of hair on my head. For instance, after three years of marriage, I've finally learned that our trashcan isn't going to take itself out on Sunday nights and that I'm tired of sleeping on the couch.

I forgive my mother for instilling me with false hope. She was only doing her job. My only hope is that she forgives me for being too lazy to diligently pursue my dreams. While some people who know me could make a compelling argument that I am still not grown up--a man-child, if you will--I am now in my 30s and most of my dreams have no chance of becoming reality. My dream of becoming a professional break-dancer will not come true because my stomach is too large and my back too fragile to perform the moves necessary to please a crowd; my dream of becoming a professional baseball player will not come true because, even though the older I get, the better I was, I was never that good to begin with; and my dream of becoming an underwear model will not come true because that is no longer a dream of mine. I could not look at myself in the mirror, or my friends and family in the eye, if I were an underwear model.

I still dream. I would like to have the temerity to speed up at yellow lights instead of slowing down; I want Will Shortz to accept one of my entries for the *New York Times* Saturday crossword puzzle; I want to live in a world in which no one says "having said that" or "that being said," or any variation thereof; and I want the bowling term for three consecutive strikes to be changed from "Turkey" to "Turney." However, at the top of my dream list is to be a nice, happy bald man. When the going gets tough, the tough get going and life is too short to sweat the small stuff--and to spout off too many clichés. I shall use short men as motivation for attaining my goal of being a nice, happy bald man.

There are many short men who are deemed to suffer from a Napoleon complex. The Napoleon complex is so named because the French Emperor, Napoleon Bonaparte--a man who stood 5'6"--was alleged to have overcompensated for his short stature by angrily waging war against other European countries and craving world domination in the late 17th and early 18th centuries. Thus, a modern angry short man who overcompensates is said to have a Napoleon complex. He doesn't necessarily want to invade England, but he's got a chip on his shoulder that negatively impacts his interactions with people and his approach to life. There is nothing wrong with being vertically challenged, but one's short stature is probably the first characteristic that is noticed in a society obsessed with physical appearances. So if you are short, you might as well slap a smile on your face. It may be cool to have power like Napoleon once did, but his thirst for power became his downfall and he wound up exiled on the island of Saint Helena. Short men beware.

I do not believe there is an equivalent psychological term to refer to angry or self-conscious bald men. And I do not want to attempt to coin one here lest I arm the world-- or at least the three people who read this book--with ammunition against the bald. Instead, I will do my part to let the world know that bald men can be happy and confident. So, when there are but a few hairs sheltering my head and Bradley Cooper, or some other man with gorgeous hair, cuts me off on the road, I will keep my middle finger in its holster, smile, and act like I don't have a care in the world. Bradley will say, *"Man, that guy is bald but he sure is nice and happy. I won't cut off any bald men again."*

I shall be known as a nice, happy bald man, and by making a positive first impression on those I meet, the fully-haired people of the world will not be afraid to interact with bald strangers and will not treat us as second-class citizens. That's the least I can do.

While many of my other dreams have gone up in flames, I owe it to myself and to others who are losing, or have lost, their hair, to be a nice, happy bald man. This is one dream I *can* make come true. After all, I don't want my mom to be a complete liar.

Epilogue

Oh, what a journey it has been so far. You know, I've heard that that which does not kill us makes us stronger. It was either Nietzsche or Kelly Clarkson who said that. Well, guess what: I'm losing my hair, but I'm still standing. And, not only that, I'm getting stronger by the day.

Sure, I have hit the occasional pothole and taken a wrong turn or two on my journey to baldness. There were all those misguided attempts I made to cover up my male pattern baldness, like the monthly trips I took to the pharmacy to pick up my prescription for *Propecia* and my exhausting morning ritual involving the "cascade effect." There were my self-serving attempts to make myself feel better about losing my hair, like the "preemptive action" strategy I deployed lo those many years. And, let's not forget about all those desperate subway rides I took as I stalked bald men in search of the perfect bald head, because I couldn't just like me for me.

But I believe I am finally on the right path. That path is acceptance. It took some imaginary friends, the Bible, my father, and a fat lady to show me that acceptance is the only cure for baldness. And now it is up to me to practice what they preach and not forget their words of wisdom as I lose more hair. I would counsel other members of the baldness community to do the same. Together we can make a difference.

As I was putting the finishing touches on this book at the library a few months ago, a young boy cautiously approached me. He couldn't have been more than six or seven years old. I don't know

An Eagle Soars

if he was lost or just looking for a friend, but I had a case of writer's block and needed a break, so I offered him a lollipop and the seat next to me. "Gee! Thanks, mister!," he said appreciatively. As he attempted to find out how many licks it really takes to get to the center of the cherry Tootsie Pop he was so thoroughly enjoying, he asked me what I was doing. "Well, son, I'm writing a book," I said matter-of-factly. "Oh. What about, mister?" Flattered by his genuine interest in me, but unsure how much a little boy knows about male pattern baldness, I simply explained to him that it's a book about how a man can lose some hair on his head and still enjoy life.

You know, fate is a funny thing. And I just had to chuckle gratefully to myself, as I knew some higher power had brought an unattended young boy and a strange man with spare lollipops in his pocket together that day. Because that young boy--bless his heart--knew exactly what I was talking about. "You know, mister, my dad is bald, and he's always in a bad mood. He misses my baseball games and he isn't nice to my mommy. When he thinks I'm asleep at night, I can hear him crying. I just know he's upset about not having any hair. Maybe you can help him, mister."

Maybe I can, son, maybe I can. Here's what I would say to that young boy's father and to anyone else who would listen: don't let male pattern baldness get you down. Be a father to your sons. Be a husband to your wives. In short, be a man.

If we can just accept the fact that we are losing our hair, we can then take the necessary steps to help the non-bald accept us as equals. We can hold doors open for women without the pretext of checking them out as they walk by. We can help senior citizens carry their groceries to the parking lot instead of pushing them out of the way because they move too slowly. We can stop wearing jean shorts in public. We can resist the temptation to sign up our children for accordion lessons, because that is child abuse. And, we can vow to never, ever say, "don't go there."

We must navigate the streets as confidently as the hungry lion that spots a lame wildebeest in the Serengeti. We must be comfortable in our own skin, and not just because there is more for the world to see. And we must just say no to toupees, hair plugs, *Propecia, Rogaine,* and berets in order to let the world know that we are losing our hair and we are not afraid to show it. That's right, we must throw our hands in the air and wave them like we just don't care.

If we can do these things, we can come that much closer to gaining the respect and acceptance of the non-bald world. We can show the fully haired that we are good people despite our lack of hair, that when we are cut, we, too, bleed. They will appreciate our effort, and remember that one good turn deserves another. Therefore, the haired people will not point and whisper as we walk down the street; they will pick us up if we fall down; they will invite us to the beach to play Pro Kadima instead of kicking sand in our faces; and they will love us for who we are, not the amount of hair we have on our heads.

People will probably say that I am doing for bald men what Betty Friedan did for women or Rosa Parks did for African-Americans. That's a good feeling, but I'm not in this for pats on the back. I'm just a regular guy who's lost some hair and bared his soul in order to try to make the world a better place for bald men.

Indeed, the nature of my fight against baldness has changed. I have given up the fight to preserve my hair with costly products and whimsical hopes for a medical cure for baldness. Instead, I have picked a new fight--the fight to make baldness acceptable to those who suffer from it and those who do not. Because, in the end, I want my tombstone to read: "Here lies Turney Hall. He had male pattern baldness, but we loved him anyway."

Sure, some day in the not-so-distant future some mad scientist is going to use stem cells to eradicate male pattern baldness. But that day has yet to come. Therefore, for my next act I shall storm into the barbershop and demand The Anton Chigurh. After that, I shall let my hair fall where it may, or fire it before it can all quit on me. Either way, I shall soar through the rest of my journey to baldness.